W9-BOA-061

Hiking
Vermont

Larry Pletcher

FALCON®

HELENA, MONTANA

A FALCONGUIDE®

Falcon® Publishing is continually expanding its list of recreational guidebooks. All books include detailed descriptions, accurate maps, and all information necessary for enjoyable trips. You can order extra copies of this book and get information and prices for other Falcon® books by writing Falcon, P.O. Box 1718, Helena, MT 59624, or by calling toll-free 1-800-582-2665. Also, please ask for a copy of our current catalog. Visit our website at www.Falcon.com or contact us by e-mail at falcon@falcon.com.

Copyright ©1996 by The Globe Pequot Press
Printed in the United States of America

4 5 6 7 8 9 10 MG 04 03 02 01 00

All rights reserved. No part of this book may be reproduced or transmitted in any form by any means, electronic or mechanical, including photocopying and recording, or by any information storage and retrieval system, except as may be expressly permitted by the 1976 Copyright Act or by the publisher. Requests for permission should be made in writing to The Globe Pequot Press, P.O. Box 480, Guilford, Connecticut, 06437.

Falcon and FalconGuide are registered trademarks of Falcon® Publishing, Inc.

All black-and-white photos by author.
Cover photo by Jerry LeBlond.

Library of Congress Cataloging-in-Publication Data

Pletcher, Larry, 1946-
   Hiking Vermont / by Larry Pletcher.
      p. cm.
   ISBN 1-56044-395-2 (pbk.)
      1. Hiking—Vermont—Guidebooks. 2. Trails—Vermont—Guidebooks.
3. Vermont—Guidebooks. I. Title.
GV199.42.V4P54 1996
796.5'1'09743—dc20   96-30389
                                                              CIP

CAUTION

Outdoor recreation activities are by their very nature potentially hazardous. All participants in such activities must assume the responsibility for their own actions and safety. The information contained in this guidebook cannot replace sound judgment and good decision-making skills, which help reduce risk exposure, nor does the scope of this book allow for disclosure of all the potential hazards and risks involved in such activities.

Learn as much as possible about the outdoor recreation activities in which you participate, prepare for the unexpected, and be cautious. The reward will be a safer and more enjoyable experience.

♻ Text pages printed on recycled paper.

CONTENTS

Acknowledgments vi
Map Legend vi
Hike Locations.. vii
Introduction 1
    Backcountry Basics 2
    Enjoying the Trail.. 10
    The Long Trail 14

THE HIKES

The Green Mountain National Forest, Southern Section 15
    1. Stratton Mountain and Stratton Pond 16
    2. Harmon Hill 20
    3. Bald Mountain, Bennington 22
    4. Haystack Mountain 25
    5. Little Rock Pond and Green Mountain 28
    6. Big Branch Brook, Griffith Lake, and Baker Peak 31
    7. Lye Brook Wilderness 35
    8. Prospect Rock, Manchester 38
    9. White Rocks National Recreation Area, Ice Beds Trail 41

The Taconic Range 43
    10. Mount Equinox, Burr and Burton Trail 44
    11. Merck Forest and Farmland Center 47

The Southern Uplands 50
    12. Amity Pond Natural Area 51
    13. Bald Mountain, Townshend 54
    14. Eshqua Bog Natural Area 57
    15. Ledges Overlook Trail 60
    16. Okemo Mountain, Healdville Trail................................ 62
    17. Mount Tom, Faulkner Trail 65

The Green Mountain National Forest, Northern Section..... 67

18. Abbey Pond 68

19. Cooley Glen and Emily Proctor Trails 71

20. Robert Frost Interpretive Trail 74

21. Mount Horrid and the Great Cliff 76

22. Monroe Skyline, Lincoln Gap to Appalachian Gap 78

23. Rattlesnake Cliffs, the Falls of Lana, and Silver Lake 81

24. Skylight Pond Trail, Battell and Bread Loaf Mountains 85

25. Texas Falls Recreation Area 88

The Champlain Lowlands 90

26. Ethan Allen Homestead, Peninsula Trail 90

27. Button Bay State Park 93

28. Green Mountain Audubon Nature Center, Sensory Trail .. 96

29. Mount Independence, Orange Trail 98

30. LaPlatte River Marsh Natural Area 101

31. Missisquoi National Wildlife Refuge,
    Black and Maquam Creek Trails 104

32. Mount Philo State Park 108

33. Red Rocks Park 110

34. Shaw Mountain Natural Area 112

The Connecticut Valley 114

35. Mount Ascutney, Weathersfield Trail 115

36. Black Mountain Natural Area 118

37. Fort Dummer State Park, Sunrise Trail 121

38. Mount Monadnock 123

39. Wilgus State Park, The Pinnacle 126

The High Five 128

40. Mount Mansfield, Sunset Ridge Trail 129

41. Killington Peak, Bucklin Trail 133

42. Mount Ellen, Jerusalem Trail 135

43. Camel's Hump, Forestry, Dean and Long Trails Loop 138

44. Mount Abraham, Battell Trail 142

The Worcester Range **144**

   45. Mount Hunger, Waterbury Trail 145

   46. Stowe Pinnacle 148

   47. Mount Worcester 150

   48. Mount Elmore 153

The Northern Uplands **156**

   49. Barr Hill Nature Preserve 156

   50. Groton State Forest, Kettle Pond, and Owls Head.......... 159

   51. Spruce Mountain 162

The Northern Border **164**

   52. Burnt Mountain 165

   53. Jay Peak 167

   54. Mount Norris 170

   55. Ritterbush Pond and Devil's Gulch 173

The Northeast Kingdom **176**

   56. Burke Mountain 177

   57. Mount Pisgah 180

   58. Mount Hor, Herbert Hawkes Trail 183

   59. Bill Sladyk Wildlife Management Area 186

   60. Wenlock Wildlife Management Area, Moose Bog 189

   61. Wheeler Mountain 193

Appendix A— USDA Forest Service Offices 196
Appendix B—Vermont Agency of Natural Resources 196
About the Author 197

ACKNOWLEDGMENTS

Folks who work to preserve and protect the trailside environment tend to be a cheerful lot. The generous assistance of local representatives from the federal, state, and private agencies that manage our forests and parks added greatly to the pleasure of writing this hiking guide. This volume, and the welcoming trails of Vermont, would suffer substantial loss without their contribution.

The political climate of the day, however, compels less conventional acknowledgments. While environmental protections are under attack in the winter of 1996, I continually thank people I never knew who long ago possessed the wisdom to set aside vast acres of Green Mountain National Forest and State of Vermont preserves. Today, concerned hikers need to make their voices heard on a national level if future generations are to judge our stewardship of the environment with equal gratitude.

MAP LEGEND

Trail	Picnic Area	Shelter
Secondary Trail	Campground	Boardwalk
Interstate	Interstate (888)	Mountain
Paved Road	U.S. Highway (88)	Cliff Edge/Outcrop
Woods Road (Non-Vehicular)	State Highway (88) (88)	State Line, Forest, Park, or Wilderness Boundary
Gravel/Graded Road	Forest Road (88)	
Bridge	Parking	Waterway
Town	Gate	Falls or Cascade
Viewpoint	Railroad Tracks	Lake/Bay/Reservoir
Structure	Firetower	Marsh

HIKE LOCATIONS MAP

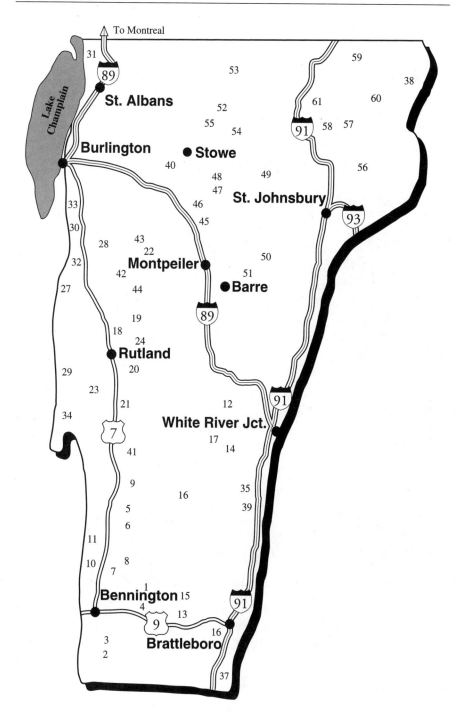

A Long Trail approach to Camel's Hump.

INTRODUCTION

If image were everything, Vermont would be nothing but mountains. Tightly packed with steep-sided hills, boisterous summits, and pristine alpine peaks, this vertical state dazzles hikers with precipitous mountain gaps, crystal rivers in serpentine valleys, and quaint crossroads villages huddled below skiable peaks. First impressions are appealing, but the mountainous face of Vermont masks a wealth of hidden hiking options. When you think of Vermont also envision lakes, history, pastoral landscapes, glacier-carved valleys, and wilderness bogs; spruce-fir forests teeming with wildlife, ponds, islands, and secluded marshes; views that are vast, wonders that are tiny; and a lake so large you'll swear it's the sea.

Hiking Vermont introduces hikers to all of the state, from the soaring tip of Camel's Hump to the quiet silence of Amity Pond and the sweep of Lake Champlain. Pick a hike, join the fun, and you'll quickly discover that there's more to this state than mountains. With the assistance of this guide, you'll trek to campsites under the pines on the shore of Silver Lake, or walk to ponds brimming with trout far north on Canada's border. Gain insights of history on urban greenways along the Winooski River, or seek moose, bobcat, deer, and otter in the Northeast Kingdom's upland terrain. Exploring vernal pools, peatland fens, or marshes bustling with wildlife, you're sure to delight in Vermont's wealth of unsung pleasures.

The rich mix of trails described here also unlocks a realm of natural wonders that readily accommodates the young or old, the physically challenged, the experienced hiker, or the novice. Nature centers and interpretive trails entertain and educate children, while rambles in boreal forests and backpacks to comfortable shelters will please the entire family. From barrier-free access to a fishing hole on the banks of a mountain stream to strenuous backpacks on secluded ponds in the heart of national forest, this FalconGuide describes a broad assortment of varied trails to match any outdoor interest.

Of course, it also includes mountain paths. Vermont's alpine treks offer another level of hiking excitement, traversing an astounding array of high terrain. Walk the Precambrian Green Mountain spine to Canada's border. Climb a peak in the Taconic Range, which extends into New York. Stroll beyond a gravel beach to an island in an ancient sea. Scale monadnocks that survived erosion above the Connecticut River. Falcons and forests, waterfalls and wilderness await hikers in these alpine regions where winter comes early and stays late, and where explorations can last mere hours or extended, mellow days.

To aid readers in pre-hike planning, this book divides the abundant resources of Vermont into eleven natural regions that reflect the state's major geographic features. Trails have been selected for the broadest range of options in each distinctive region. Readers will find backpacks and day trips throughout Vermont, and parents can locate adventures for children in any

1

part of the state. Experienced hikers can find challenging outings near the gentle Connecticut Valley, while beginners can select easy walks amidst imposing Green Mountain peaks. Quick-reference difficulty ratings, trail highlights, individual maps, and descriptions convey the feel of each hike and provide valuable tools for choosing trips that suit each hiker's needs.

Before exploring pristine bogs or windswept alpine peaks, remember that each hiker is responsible for maintaining his or her personal safety and the integrity of the environment he or she seeks. This guide reviews basic requirements, clothing, equipment, and preparation needed to safely hike diverse habitats and elevations where quirky weather can bring a thundering downpour or a tranquil summer breeze. Throughout Vermont, delicate wetlands, eroding hillsides, and unique alpine zones demand that hikers walk softly and cautiously. This guide also provides tips on current regulations and overnight options to help you enjoy your trip. Be aware of the sensitive environment, current regulations, and overnight options. Sections of this guide will help.

Vermont is a compact state. Each bump in its landscape or twist in its roads leads to bright discoveries. This book is designed to guide your quest for the secrets of its varied trails that lie around the next corner or beyond a nearby hill.

BACKCOUNTRY BASICS

THINGS TO KNOW BEFORE YOU GO

Vermonters share a Yankee reputation for practical wisdom and common sense, two terrific qualities for roaming New England trails. Sensible, well-prepared hikers have little to fear while exploring this marvelous state. Boulder-strewn slopes, cascading streams, and unpredictable weather don't always make for safe environments, but hikers who know their own limits— and expect the unexpected—soon count these ordinary challenges among the joys of backcountry travel. Whether spying on moose in reclusive bogs or tramping the Long Trail at alpine heights, competent hikers anticipate problems and pack sound judgment on each trail that they wander.

Most of Vermont's vast assortment of trails pose little danger, but several adventurous routes could lead inexperienced hikers into serious harm, including hypothermia, disorientation, or physical injury. Each hiker bears responsibility for knowing the character of a planned hike. What equipment will you need on specific trails? What can be expected from changeable weather? What critters will you meet, and where can you camp without harming the environment? The next few pages will help you assess the demands of particular hikes and anticipate problems that may arise. Be ready to enjoy the trails of Vermont with knowledge and confidence.

PREPARATION

Thoughtful preparation is the cornerstone of safe hiking. But "safe hiking" is a relative concept—there are no guarantees out there, and hikers of varying capacities will be happy with different levels of preparation. The bottom line is to make sure that your clothing and equipment stand up to the conditions you're likely to meet.

Each trail described in this guide begins with basic information that's useful in planning your hike. Difficulty ratings are reliable first indicators of the level of preparation required. Also consult the general description, general location, length, and elevation gain headings for an expanded assessment of the character of the trail, how remote or exposed it may be, and the nature of its terrain.

"Easy" trails are short routes over gentle grades that require little equipment or preparation. Sturdy walking shoes are all you need to enjoy these

Red trillium, vibrant accent in the springtime woods.

peaceful trails, accessible to any hiker. Depending on weather, a water bottle and rain jacket might make your trip more comfortable, and bug dope will be a welcome addition at certain times of year.

"Moderate" trails cover a wider range and necessitate more preparation. Although distances, elevation gains, and grades are increased on these routes, moderate hikes are comfortable outings for average hikers. Paths may be rocky and rough, however, and light hiking boots are recommended as minimal footwear. A small day pack holding insect repellent, rain protection, drinking water, and quick-energy snacks should be part of your basic gear. A guidebook, trail map, lunch, and light wool sweater should also find their way into your pack.

"Intermediate" trails offer vigorous exercise. Reasonably fit hikers will know they've had a workout, and sedentary types will find themselves stopping often to catch their breath. On these trails, sturdy hiking boots are highly recommended. The same items carried on moderate hikes may suffice, but the majority of these routes cross over the line where such limited preparation is simply not enough.

You can sprain an ankle or catch a chill on even an easy hike, but beyond a certain limit trails become too rough and remote for you not to be ready for the consequences. I make it a habit to carry a full complement of day-hiking gear once the round-trip distance exceeds 3 miles or the gain in elevation approaches 1,200 feet. A moderate pack holds a camera and other good stuff that I like to carry, and I can forge ahead on misty trails when I know that my pack holds all of the following:

- hooded rain jacket
- rain pants
- wool hat
- wool sweater
- light long-sleeved shirt
- map
- compass
- small flashlight
- toilet paper
- waterproof matches

- fleece jacket (optional in midsummer)
- waterproof pack cover
- wool mittens
- extra T-shirt
- guidebook
- multi-function knife
- two 1-quart plastic water bottles
- insect repellent
- first-aid kit

- lunch (or enough trail snacks to make a meal if necessary)

No doubt many of these items are already in your closet, but be cautious of substitutions and don't skimp on the basic list. It's important that standby clothing be wool or synthetic to wick moisture away from the skin. Avoid blue jeans and cotton garments that hold the water in, inviting hypothermia whenever they're wet.

The first-aid kit doesn't have to be a commercial package. Mine's just a waterproof plastic box that holds an assortment of bandages (small to large butterfly type), tape, gauze, antibacterial ointment, elastic bandage, personal medications, and aspirin (or acetaminophen if you hike with children). I also choose to include a feather-light emergency thermal blanket, matches, candle, sunscreen, lip balm, and a basic first-aid chart in the same small package.

"Difficult" trails aren't recommended for every hiker. Unusually long or steep, often with tricky scrambles over slabs of rock or boulders, these hikes also generally present a higher risk of exposure to changeable weather. Don't explore these routes unless you've done a bit of hiking and think you're in good condition. Sturdy boots and a full pack, as suggested above, are essential.

Beyond clothing and equipment, you're not really prepared to tackle "intermediate" or "difficult" trails until you consider mental outlook. Remember, you're supposed to be having fun out there. No one is keeping score. If you wonder, "Are we having fun yet?" and struggle with every step, you should probably be asking yourself a few other honest questions: "Do I have a margin of safety?" and "What am I trying to prove?"

Exhaustion weakens the muscles, dulls the mind, and doesn't make for good times. For greater pleasure, safer hiking, and fewer regrets, slow down, lower your sights, and stay within your limits. Superb trails throughout Vermont explore beautiful pockets of nature within your current grasp, and fabulous views on difficult hikes can often be duplicated on gentler trails that match your present skills. Don't rush. Savor your progress and enjoy your own discoveries. Higher peaks and steeper trails will always be there on another day when you are ready for them.

Finally, classic advice about safety tells you never to hike alone. If the peaceful aura of a mountain peak or a sunset on a northern lake weren't such a compelling lure, some of us might heed this warning. Fact is, though, hiking alone can be a heck of a lot of fun. If you take the solitary route, understand the dangers, be prepared, follow a hiking plan, and leave it with someone who'll know how to react if you're overdue.

WEATHER

Autumn in Vermont is legendary. Chill mornings, crisp air, and forests blazing with color draw hikers to every corner of this state in an annual fall migration. Golden canopies of stately sugarbush, crimson leaves near quiet bogs, and burnished landscapes beneath mountain peaks make autumn walks unique, but ample pleasures also grace Vermont's other hiking seasons. April is the most eagerly awaited month, when spring breezes bring an end to winter and thaw trails in lower regions. Woodlands glow with pastel hues of buds about to burst, and carpets of wildflowers brightly emerge for their season in the sun. With mild days, cool nights, and frequent infusions of dry Canadian air, summer avoids extended bouts of heat and humidity that make hiking a steamy affair. Long summer days are perfectly suited for exploring alpine heights, meandering through forests of pungent pine, or camping by a cooling lake.

Unfortunately, this varied climate also has difficulty settling down. "If you don't like the weather, just wait a minute," sums up the local wisdom. At a confluence of jet stream patterns, New England's location makes forecasting an adventure, and predictions a question of odds. Vermont's quirky nature also implies that conditions in the Northeast Kingdom have little bearing on the weather in Brattleboro, and that neither has any relationship to what's happening on Abraham's Peak. Far from being a problem, smart hikers view the shifting weather as a recreational buffet. Check the forecasts, skim *Hiking Vermont* for good trails with favorable weather, and be prepared if conditions change.

Hypothermia and lightning are common dangers for hikers everywhere, but visitors to the highest Green Mountain elevations have added reason to take care. Prevailing northwest winds sweep across the Champlain Basin to meet their first resistance on Vermont's majestic peaks. Inexperienced hikers quickly learn that refreshing valley weather can translate into dangerous conditions on a blustery mountaintop. Remember, hypothermia is more than a winter problem. Even on pleasant summer days, a sweaty climb up a mountain trail, strong wind, and temperatures in the 50s spell trouble for ill-equipped hikers. Rain, drizzle, or encounters with damp shrubs will magnify the problem, quickly leading to the loss of body core temperature. To protect yourself from danger, expect chill winds at higher elevations, layer your clothing, always carry raingear, and return to lower altitudes when your inner voice tells you you're pushing your luck.

Strong winds also sweep clouds across the summits, bringing cold fronts with thunder, lightning, and downpours to relieve the heat of summer days. It's astounding how many hikers push on toward waiting peaks in spite of dangerous steel gray clouds that ominously rumble. Nature is bountiful, and hiking can be a pleasure if you keep your ego in check. You don't have to reach the top; storms permit time for sensible retreat on most trails in this state, without increasing your exposure to the risk of lightning strikes. If storms are in the offing, or you're cold, wet, and tired, turn back, lose altitude, get away from exposed positions, and seek protection in the sheltering forest. You can always conquer the summit on a more hospitable day.

Finally, remember that New England has its own special season. Between the close of winter and the beginning of spring, "mud season" turns trails wet and sloppy or clogs them with pockets of hidden snow. Under these conditions, footsteps on steeper routes cause rapid erosion and severely degrade the trail. Instead of harming the environment during this mucky time of year, review this guidebook for suggested trails that can be enjoyed with clean boots and a clear conscience.

BUGS, BEASTS, AND NOXIOUS CRITTERS

Black flies are the worst and most persistent. These tiny monsters draw blood if given the chance, but reports that swarms carry hikers away have yet to be verified. Emerging first in early May, black flies continue to hatch through the middle of June at higher latitudes and elevations. The best protection is any good product containing DEET, but you'll often catch a whiff of hikers experimenting with their own solutions. Strong winds and lack of cover help drive these critters away as well as the mosquitoes that arrive a

Stillwater Brook, Groton State Forest.

few weeks later. In any event, the worst of both plagues generally ends by mid-July.

Deer ticks carry Lyme disease with its flu-like symptoms of fever, chills, fatigue, body aches, distinctive bull's-eye rash, and long-term, severe complications if left untreated. The illness is rare in Vermont, with fewer than a handful of indigenous cases confirmed each year. To take precautions, cover legs with long pants and spray with a repellent containing DEET, especially when hiking in grassy, wooded, or brushy areas outside of the high peaks. The pinhead-sized tick must remain on your body for many hours to transmit the disease. Do an inspection after your hike and remove ticks with tweezers as soon as you can.

Giardia lamblia is an intestinal parasite that could be lurking in any surface water. Do not drink from streams, lakes, or rivers without first taking appropriate precautions. Purify drinking water by treatment, adequate filtration, or boiling for 5 minutes to avoid delayed onset of severe cramps and diarrhea that require medical attention.

For most hikers, spotting a black bear or moose is the highlight of a special day. Neither animal is normally aggressive, and moose in particular seem indifferent to human spying. Still, there are times when either of these critters could place you in a real dilemma. A nearsighted bull moose becomes disagreeable when he's cruising for a mate, and he may not always comprehend that you're not his natural rival. A mother moose with calf is equally jumpy. Black bears are dangerous if they sense you threaten their young, and some become belligerent if they're accustomed to dining on camp food. A few simple rules keep both people and animals safe: Don't antagonize wildlife, and keep a respectful distance. If you're camping overnight, always hang your food pack, and give a call to the nearest USDA Forest Service office to avoid campsites where bears have been a problem.

Regrettably, even small woodland critters have recently become dangerous to humans. The mid-Atlantic strain of rabies has already spread into southern Vermont, causing dramatic increases in the incidence of this disease in the early 1990s. Raccoons, foxes, skunks, and other small mammals carry the disease. Don't touch or pet wild animals, and avoid creatures that act strangly or unusually aggressive. Bites that break the skin bring danger of exposure to the disease, as do contaminated cuts, open wounds, or mucous membranes contaiminated by the saliva or neural tissue of an infected animal. If you've been exposed in such a way, to an animal that may be rapid, you will require vaccination. If left untreated until symptoms develop, rabies is always fatal.

WILDERNESS AREAS, PRIMITIVE CAMPING, AND STATE REGULATIONS

More than 350,000 acres of national forest blanket the mountains of central and southern Vermont, a verdant natural treasure. Stretching 120 miles north from the Massachusetts border astride a chain of alpine peaks, the Green Mountain National Forest encompasses six wilderness areas, more than 500 miles of hiking trails, and countless backcountry pleasures. Divided near Rutland into northern and southern halves, this vast federal preserve boasts such a patchwork quilt of outdoor options that newcomers can easily be confused about their choices.

In this neck of the woods, the term "primitive camping" is used to describe overnight stays outside of established campgrounds. Simple huts and three-sided shelters distributed near the Long Trail, secluded campsites accessed by trails or forest roads, and your own perfect spot in a pristine wilderness all fit this definition. Vermont's abundance of overnight options is a boon to backcountry hikers, but backpackers need to understand the details of local regulations.

Fire permits are not required if you're camping on federal land, but some of the property within the bounds of the national forest is private, not federally owned. Since you're legally required to have the owner's permission to camp on private property, backpackers striking out on their own need to pay very close attention to maps and boundary markers, and know exactly where they stand. Restrictions on camping near various geographic features also differ throughout the national forest, but you'll satisfy the most stringent regulations and observe good camping practices if you always locate your campsite and tend to sanitation at least 200 feet from trails, roads, and water sources. Other logical limitations should be self-imposed by hikers with a conscience. To minimize the impact of heavy use even on federal land, camping is discouraged within the Long Trail corridor except at established shelters. Many hikers also consider open fires needlessly destructive to the forest, and virtually everyone regards camping on fragile mountaintops as downright antisocial. Carry a backpacker's stove, build a fire only if a ring is provided, and be thoughtful of the environment when selecting an overnight site.

The six wilderness areas that pepper Green Mountain National Forest are also governed by the Wilderness Act, which precludes motorized or mechanical equipment within nearly 60,000 acres. Independent types will relish these rugged tracts where hiking trails are limited and mountain bikers need not apply. Whatever your plans, it's good policy to touch base with the local USDA Forest Service ranger district office before venturing into the national forest. (See Appendix A for a list of USDA Forest Service offices.)

State regulation is equally complex, and in some cases more restrictive. Superb backpacking is readily available in many of Vermont's public parks and forests, but regulations are more detailed than in the federal jurisdictions. "Zero Impact" camping methods, specific clearances from water, roads, trails, and structures, prohibitions against camping above 2,500 feet, limits to group size and composition, and number of consecutive camping nights are a few of the comprehensive provisions written into law. Also be aware that outings in state parks subject hikers to day-use fees if the park is open. For a list of the many public lands where primitive camping is allowed, complete regulations, seasonal park services, and applicable fees, contact

contact one of the offices of the Vermont Department of Forests, Parks and Recreation listed in Appendix B.

RESPECTING THE LAND

Good news! Most hikers finally understand that a spirit of backcountry freedom doesn't leave room for selfish behavior. Responsible hikers know that you don't toss candy wrappers on the trail, drop food scraps in the woods, leave cigarette butts at campsites, cut trees for firewood, trench your tent, wash in streams, or otherwise act like boors. The basics have been learned. Now it's time to move along. As the twentieth century ends, respecting the land has come to mean more than simply not trashing the place.

In an age of spiraling populations, regulatory reform, cost/benefit analysis, and focus on the bottom line, anyone who finds renewal on a woodland trail needs to get involved in the conservation effort. Join your local hiking club, conservation organization, or interest group of choice. Support efforts to maintain forests and mountains in more than isolated preserves, to ensure that the natural gifts we've inherited continue to survive. As you hike from day to day, leave the trail in better condition than when you arrived. Carry out everything you carry in, and pick up after any hikers who forget this obligation. Finally, while enjoying the blessings of this irreplaceable land, remember that thoughtless footsteps often cause enduring damage.

Vermont's windswept summits comprise arctic worlds of delicate vegetation typical of regions hundreds of miles north. At lower elevations, unremarkable to the untrained eye, marshes and bogs blossom with descendants of plants left by retreating glaciers 10,000 years ago. Obeying the credo of "Pack It In-Pack It Out" isn't enough to save such fragile environments in an age of heavy traffic. Consider the impact of your visit, and please stay on the trail. In most areas you'll prevent erosion. In a few special places, you'll save rare varieties of plants that grow slowly in harsh environments and rapidly succumb to the tread of boot-clad feet. Walk softly in these magical realms, where even the imprint of a foot should not be left behind.

ENJOYING THE TRAIL

The beauty of a rocky peak, or the mystery of a path unknown. A glimpse of waterfowl on a hidden pond, or a chance to photograph springtime blossoms on a misty forest floor. However you define contentment, an abundance of outdoor pleasures await you in this compact state. Whatever your age or experience, trails in Vermont beckon with a lot of fun. The information that follows is meant to help everyone enjoy hiking here even more.

HIKING WITH CHILDREN

Nothing beats hiking with children. Resilient and enthusiastic, kids have a knack for opening our eyes to enchantment, adding a special luster to the pleasures of the trail. With proper handling, kids are also pretty tough. The trick is to start them early and bring them along at a steady pace. Even if toddlers snooze most of the time, they absorb the rhythm of hiking while bouncing along on your back. Keep hikes comfortably within their limits as kids continue to grow, and a natural progression soon results in confident older children wondering why parents lag behind climbing a rigorous peak.

If you haven't started early, a few tricks can turn even hesitant children into eager, happy companions. First, encourage their sense of pride. Also, hikers of any age require adequate, safe equipment. To keep up with adults, kids need raingear, extra clothing, and more on their feet than sneakers. Decent boots, their own water bottle, and even a child-sized pack will work wonders on the trail. Aside from safer hiking, enthusiasm soars if kids are treated with the same respect as grown-up hikers.

Both children and adults need to stop often to replenish themselves with fluids and high-energy snacks. Most kids think of these breaks as rewards for active hiking. Fruit juice and healthy foods are fine fuels for any child, but keep in mind that a shameless bribe of chocolate will quickly perk up any kid having a rare bad day.

If all else fails and your child is a balky hiker, try teaming up with other children. Kids accomplish amazing feats when they're engaged in busy chatter with a gaggle of newfound friends. Nature centers, school groups, hiking clubs, conservation organizations, or your local YMCA or YWCA are great places to find family walks, other parents with common interests, or environmental discovery programs specially designed to intrigue kids.

Vermont abounds with great family hikes, and a large number of state facilities cater to younger children. Button Bay State Park and Groton State Forest are just two popular destinations offering nature trails, nature centers, and swimming holes that prove irresistable to children. For a real change of pace, the Merck Forest and Farmland Center delights kids and parents too with hiking trails, campsites, a sugar shack, and farm animals for close, hands-on inspection. As time goes on, experienced kids will be happy exploring the same trails that attract their parents. The sweeping vistas of Camel's Hump and a campsite under the pines convey a sense of wonder to hikers of any age. Check the general description at the beginning of each hike in this guide to identify the broad selection of distinctive trails that make ideal family outings.

HIKES FOR THE PHYSICALLY CHALLENGED

Throughout the Green Mountain State, unique facilities open pathways to nature for those who are physically challenged. Fishing access to a mountain stream, numerous wooded campsites, a nature center near Lake Champlain, and the state's preeminent historical homestead are all barrier-

Tranquil hiking on Worcester Mountain.

free. The visually impaired, as well as curious sighted hikers, can also follow one exceptional trail that calls upon other senses to encounter the environment.

People with more limited disabilities will be able to enjoy several trails and related facilities included in this guide. Short paths to viewpoints over bogs or natural areas, convenient nature centers, and easy walks throughout the state provide ready access to the great outdoors for many who are physically challenged. In a few spectacular places, hiking trails may prove inaccessible to people with disabilities, but picnic sites and opulent vistas can be leisurely enjoyed. Mount Equinox, Mount Philo, and the impressive summit of Mount Mansfield are among the dramatic locations where auto roads rise above surrounding forests to high-altitude overlooks that can be shared by any hiker. The general description at the beginning of each hike in this guide highlights locations with special facilities for the physically challenged. Check the difficulty rating and full hike description to find other trails that may be suitable for persons with limited disabilities.

HUTS AND SHELTERS

Unlike its White Mountain neighbors, the indulgent pleasures of catered huts aren't available in Vermont. To make up for this lack of luxury, though, rustic cabins and simple shelters lavishly adorn the entire length of the Green Mountain State. An overnight backpack here can be a simple local affair, without the bother of long-distance travel to the base of a northern peak.

The Appalachian Trail and Long Trail are prominent in Vermont, so shelters are never more than a few miles apart atop the Green Mountain crest. You'll find everything from log cabins to A-frame huts at many of these locations, but the Adirondack-style log lean-to is the typical accommodation. Fire rings and pit toilets are usually provided. Water is often close by. Unless you plan to visit a popular spot on a busy summer weekend, shelters generally eliminate the need to carry a tent. Take a backpacker's stove, be ready to camp elsewhere should the need arise, and always observe the rules of no-trace camping wherever your path may lead. To help plan your trip, each hike description in this guide makes reference to any shelter within striking distance of the trail.

WILDLIFE

Vermont is loaded with wildlife, but sightings are more likely at lower elevations. Spruce grouse, ravens, random hares, and rare wandering moose might be spotted near the higher peaks, but large animals have little reason to compete with marvelous views. You'll find more success away from the popular summits, especially on a few of the lesser-known routes. Moose, deer, and bear are plentiful in the Northeast Kingdom, where state forests and management areas preserve deer yards, abundant range, and ample cover. Check Groton State Forest, Ritterbush Pond, the Sladyk Wildlife Management Area, and woodland trails throughout the state to spot these larger mammals, together with smaller forest creatures like fox, beaver, raccoon, fisher, and porcupine.

Birders will find success all around the state. Eshqua and Moose bogs are promising locations, or stop by the LaPlatte River marsh and the park at Button Bay for glimpses of the many species that visit Lake Champlain. While you're at it, make sure you don't miss the Missisquoi National Wildlife Refuge in the northwest corner of the state, with its migratory waterfowl.

One particular species requires a special word. A program is underway to reintroduce peregrine falcons to the mountains of Vermont. A few trails near cliffs at higher elevations may be closed or relocated from time to time to prevent hikers from intruding on the falcon's environment. Support the effort to reintegrate these gracious birds. Stay clear of sensitive nesting sites and obey all posted restrictions.

PLANTS AND TREES

What a selection! Bogs that burst with heaths and sedges, pitcher plants, and cranberries, strewn about with rare varieties of beautiful orchids. Forest glades that glow with springtime beauty, bunchberry, trillium, and tiger lilies ringed by pillared trunks speckled by the sun. Even Vermont's mountain summits are garnished in alpine splendor, with tiny lichens, club moss, and deer's hair sedge huddled in rocky crags. You don't have to be an expert to enjoy the abundance of forms and colors, but a field guide to wildflowers or plants of the arctic and alpine regions could be your introduction to a whole new world of outdoor fun.

THE LONG TRAIL

There are two kinds of hikers in Vermont: those who know all about the Long Trail, and those who haven't hiked here much. A 265-mile path that follows the thread of the Green Mountains from Massachusetts to Canada's border, this exceptional resource spans the length of Vermont and traces the course of the Appalachian Trail for more than 100 miles.

A detailed description of this celebrated trail isn't part of this guidebook because a four-week trek on a mountain path is clearly more than a hike—it's a serious expedition. The extensive planning and logistics required for sustained Long Trail commitments exceed the scope of a statewide guide that's designed for the average hiker. It's enough to fill another book, and the Green Mountain Club has published the definitive *Guide Book of the Long Trail* for nearly eighty years.

Observant readers will note, however, that disguised Long Trail descriptions permeate *Hiking Vermont*. From Harmon Hill to Jay Peak, day trip routes and feeder-path networks conspire to place the Long Trail at the heart of countless Green Mountain treks. If you've walked the slopes of Mount Mansfield, looked out over Ritterbush Pond, or visited the top of Mount Horrid, the Long Trail guided your hike.

Because of its predominance, a few facts about the Long Trail prove useful, even to casual hikers. Throughout Vermont, the Long Trail and Appalachian Trail are distinctively blazed in white, while other paths (though not all) are generally blazed in blue. In addition, each Vermont highway that spans the Green Mountain crest intersects the Long Trail at a prominently marked crossing. The path and its many trailheads are uniformly easy to find.

After venturing onto this corridor, hikers also discover that dozens of overnight shelters blanket the Long Trail route. Board huts, tent platforms, lean-tos, or log cabins are typically stationed 6 to 8 miles apart, but are often very much closer, especially when nestled near a wilderness lake or a scenic mountainside. Sooner or later, as you traipse over Green Mountain paths, the well-used track of the Long Trail will emerge as a welcome sight. In time, you may even join other hikers in regarding this distinctive trail that never strays far from shelter as an old reliable friend, instilling a sense of security when you're far away from home.

THE GREEN MOUNTAIN NATIONAL FOREST, SOUTHERN SECTION

OVERVIEW

More than 353,000 acres of the Green Mountain National Forest blanket the crest of the Green Mountain ridge from the border of Massachusetts to the northern slopes of Lincoln Mountain southwest of the town of Waitsfield. Divided near Rutland into separate halves, the southern section of this bountiful resource forms a 50-mile wedge that preserves the core of southern Vermont.

The state's highest peaks aren't found in this southern region, but four designated wilderness tracts, the White Rocks National Recreation Area, and enticing landscapes that inspired the Appalachian Trail foster a wealth

Springtime hiking at Stratton Pond.

of backcountry options conveniently close to home. Wooded peaks, wilderness ponds, and miles of marvelous hiking typify this exceptional region where backpackers choose from a selection of campsites that rank among the best in the state. Stratton Pond, Lye Brook, Little Rock Pond, and Griffith Lake attract hikers of all ages and abilities to their captivating shores for solitary day-long adventures or weekend family retreats.

1   STRATTON MOUNTAIN AND STRATTON POND

General description:	A classic day hike to fire tower views and waterfront walks on a wild pond's shore; lean-tos and tent platforms offer overnight options.
General location:	South-central Vermont, about 20 miles southeast of Manchester.
Length:	11 miles.
Difficulty:	Intermediate.
Elevation gain:	1,700 feet.
Special attractions:	Wildlife, mountain views, and camping on Stratton Pond.
Maps:	USGS Stratton Mountain quad.
For more information:	Manchester Ranger District, Routes 11 and 30, RR 1, Box 1940, Manchester Center, VT 05255; (802) 362-2307.

Finding the trailhead: From Vermont Highway 100 in West Wardsboro, turn west about 0.5 mile south of the post office and cemetery onto the unmarked Arlington-West Wardsboro Road (also known as the Kelly Stand Road). After 3.4 miles, continue straight at an intersection where Jamaica Road turns right to the Stratton Mountain Ski Area. Trailhead parking is approximately 6.8 miles from VT 100, just east of a bridge over the East Branch of the Deerfield River at the Long Trail/Appalachian Trail crossing. Portions of this road are not maintained in winter.

The hike: The inspirational source of the Long Trail (LT) and Appalachian Trail (AT), Stratton Mountain has long been regarded as hallowed hiking ground. But not until land acquisitions and trail relocations in the late 1980s was this classic route finally secured. From fire tower views on Stratton's summit to waterfront camps on a wild pond's shore, an 11-mile loop through the heart of the Green Mountain National Forest now permanently displays the diversity of Vermont's allure. Day trippers, weekend backpackers, and cross-country hikers take equal pleasure from these magical trails. Don't expect to enjoy them alone.

1 STRATTON MOUNTAIN AND STRATTON POND

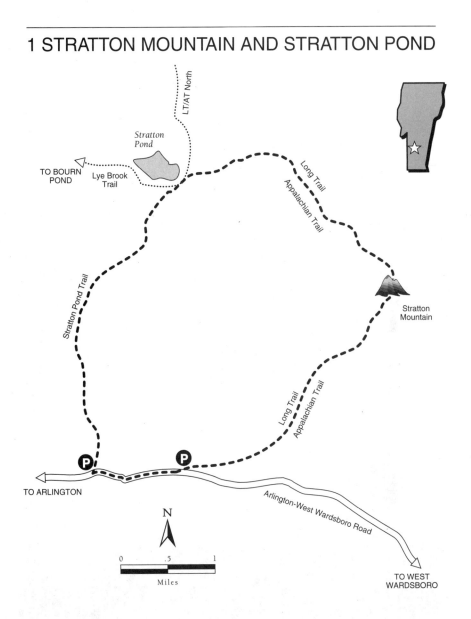

This circuitous hike neatly divides into three distinctive parts: the climb to Stratton's summit, the descent to Stratton Pond, and the woodland ramble back to the access road. The first leg follows a new portion of the LT/AT, a worn path that leaves the corner of the parking area and climbs an open slope. Spanning a grass-covered roadbed after only 0.1 mile, a directional sign points into the woods where hikers pick their way past hoofprints impressed in the mud. The route tilts upward and dries out after the first 0.25 mile, trading moose bogs for seasonal brooks and the ruts of old skidder roads.

17

A short descent ends near mossy glades and the outlet of a beaver pond before the trail resumes its gentle climb, bisecting a grove of paper birch and angling across a gravel road 1.3 miles from the trailhead. Beyond this crossing, gradients increase modestly until the path jumps a small drainage and wriggles to the north on a rockier, steeper slope. As hikers gain elevation, a filigree of hardwoods obscures summits to the left, a scenic spur passes on a switchback to the right, and the route commences a long traverse of the mountain's southwestern flank. An unmistakable view of Somerset Reservoir and the ski slopes of Mount Snow greet hikers at a trailside rest 100 yards south of a spring, just as the path begins an unexpectedly moderate zigzag, 0.6 mile from the top.

During a recent visit, throngs of hikers congregated around the fire tower on the summit, undeterred by the charred remains of a ranger's cabin a few yards south. A sunny opening encircled by evergreens that grant protection from the wind, the clearing at the base of the tower is a magnet for hikers wanting to rest or ogle the view. From the enclosed platform atop the metal tower are views of Stratton Pond fronting Mount Equinox and the sweeping Taconic Range, Mount Ascutney and Mount Monadnock rising proudly in the east, and Stratton Mountain's North Peak pointing up the Vermont Valley like the prow of a sailing ship.

The second leg of the hike begins at a faint wooden arrow that points left (northwest) a little beyond the tower. (The wide path straight ahead leads to a ski lift on North Peak.) An easy descent on this continuation of the LT/AT

The North Shore Trail skims the wetlands of Stratton Pond.

scurries past western overlooks that are being rapidly overgrown and slogs through brooks that invade the trail on the upper slopes. Inevitably the path drops more quickly down the mountain before switchbacks ease the pace, and the trail fords a rocky stream more than 1 mile below the top.

About 2.5 miles north of their first junction, the trail re-visits the gravel road it crossed while making the ascent as it launches into the most varied mile of the hike. Descending cautiously west from the road, the path ambles up and down hillocks, tramps through forest wetlands, and spans a gurgling brook 50 yards downstream from a beaver bog. From this low point in the drainage, the route eases past a marsh on the left and rises to an overlook of a larger pond on the right, both brimming with great potential for viewing wildlife. Tracking to the flat top of a moderate ridge, the second leg of the hike concludes at a major junction with the Stratton Pond Trail 3.9 miles from the access road (left) and 0.1 mile from Stratton Pond (right).

Don't even think about heading home without first turning right and exploring the extraordinary body of water that shimmers through the trees. From a clearing at the southeastern end of Stratton Pond, a combination of paths make circumnavigation easy. The Lye Brook Trail (see Hike 7) skims the southern shore, while the LT/AT passes the junction with the North Shore Trail after only 0.1 mile. For overnight hikes, caretakers supervise two rustic shelters located on the southern waterfront, and wooden platforms wait for tenters on the opposite side. Even if you don't have time to completely circle the pond, check out the eastern end of the North Shore Trail, a marvelous sojourn of blueberries, bogs, and boardwalks, rocky conifer shores, and reedy wetland marshes, a naturalist's delight.

When it's finally time to go, retrace your steps to the top of the ridge and turn right (south) on the Stratton Pond Trail for a bumpy glide back to the access road. Rising and falling through birch woods and wetland forest glades, the return route crosses a grass-covered four-wheel-drive track after 1.5 miles, flowing less up than down for the rest of the journey south. The last 100 yards drop quickly. Hikers meet the road 50 yards east of another parking lot, a good place to park a second car. If you're limited to a single vehicle, turn left (east) and follow the gravel road over the hill 1.1 miles to the original trailhead.

2   HARMON HILL

General description:	A half-day hike to a low summit overlooking Bennington, the Vermont Valley, and the Taconic Range.
General location:	East of Bennington in extreme southwestern Vermont.
Length:	3.4 miles round-trip.
Difficulty:	Moderate.
Elevation gain:	1,000 feet.
Special attractions:	Western views and wildflowers on a flat-topped ridge.
Maps:	USGS Bennington, Woodford, and Pownal quads.
For more information:	Manchester Ranger District, Routes 11 and 30, RR 1, Box 1940, Manchester Center, VT 05255; (802) 362-2307.

Finding the trailhead: A large Long Trail/Appalachian Trail (LT/AT) parking lot is located on the north side of Vermont Highway 9, 4.75 miles east of the intersection of VT 9 and U.S. Highway 7 in downtown Bennington. The trailhead is directly across the highway. Follow signs for the LT/AT south.

The hike: Easy access, superb views, an invigorating climb, and respite on a wooded ridge—little wonder that Harmon Hill is a popular local hike. Still, standing near the trailhead deep in a pass beneath opposing hills, hikers often have second thoughts as they crane their necks to spot the top of this notch's daunting pitch. It helps to know that the challenge you see is mostly the challenge you get. Once you surmount this imposing gap, the rest is a walk in the park.

Following the familiar white blazes of the Long Trail/Appalachian Trail (LT/AT), the route scrambles directly up the 0.5-mile rocky grade, gaining several hundred feet in elevation while Vermont Highway 9 rapidly recedes into the bottom of the rugged gap. Swirling steeply northwest while ascending the boisterous slope, hikers gradually lose sight of the road and focus on trillium that line the rough-cut trail like footlights on a garden path. In time, the route gently turns back on itself and heads more directly south before crude attempts at switchbacks and an abundance of stairlike stones finally carry hikers to the top of the peaceful ridge.

Descending slightly down the back side of the slope, the trail rolls along at a steady gait on a broad sun-drenched ridge where springtime carpets of white and yellow flowers add luster to the forest floor. Wooden planks cover wet patches and bogs before the path strays out of the lowlands on a long, steady rise that gradually meanders to the western edge of the ridge. Winds here signal the approaching hilltop, as do the charred remains of fires that are sometimes set to maintain the open view.

2 HARMON HILL AND 3 BALD MOUNTAIN, BENNINGTON

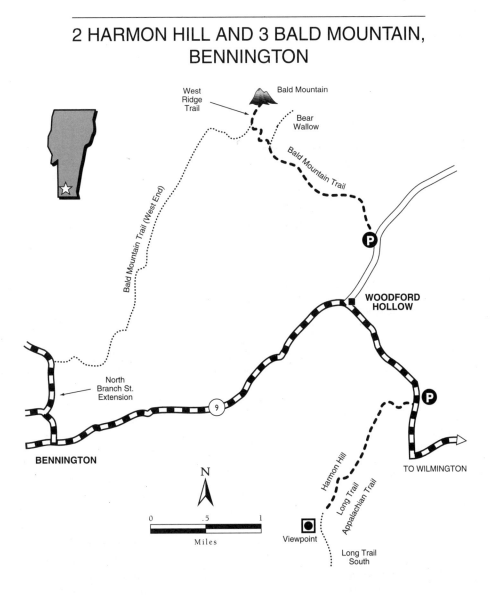

At the top of Harmon Hill, an elevation sign stands above a spacious clearing that sprawls over the lip of the sloping ridge. There's plenty of room in this grassy patch for having a snack, catching some sun, and generally lounging about while rousing yourself on occasion to appreciate the marvelous view. Bennington is prominent below, of course, with its famous Battle Monument protruding just west of town. What captures the imagination, though, is a serpentine, slender highway that spans a pastoral valley and fades into the Taconic Range with the promise of a country road.

The steep section of Harmon Hill can be dicey in wet weather. Step carefully and slow down, especially on your return. Better yet, save this hike for a clear summer morning when the sun at your back will highlight the incredible western view.

3 BALD MOUNTAIN, BENNINGTON

General description:	A half-day hike to a tree-clad summit known as Bald Mountain.
General location:	Near Woodford Hollow, 4 miles east of Bennington.
Length:	4 miles round-trip.
Difficulty:	Intermediate.
Elevation gain:	1,600 feet.
Special attractions:	Good views of the Green Mountains and the neighboring Taconic Range.
Maps:	USGS Bennington and Woodford quads.
For more information:	Manchester Ranger District, Routes 11 and 30, RR 1, Box 1940, Manchester Center, VT 05255; (802) 362-2307.

See Map on Page 21

Finding the trailhead: From the intersection of U.S. Highway 7 and Vermont Highway 9 in Bennington, travel east on VT 9, 3.75 miles and turn left (north) onto a gravel road at the Woodford Municipal Building. After crossing two bridges and passing several homes, this country road skirts a large cement water tank 0.8 mile from the highway. A trail sign marking the eastern end of the Bald Mountain Trail is off the road to the left about 20 yards past the tank. No parking lot is provided. Park carefully without blocking the road or driveways in the area.

As an alternative, the west end of the Bald Mountain Trail departs from a sharp curve on North Branch Street Extension next to an electric transmission line in suburban Bennington. From VT 9 turn north onto North Branch St. 0.75 mile east of the center of town, and then right onto North Branch St. Ext. crossing a bridge that spans the river. The western trailhead is on the right, 0.4 mile beyond the bridge.

The hike: Hiking and history merge in the southwest corner of Vermont, where the famous Bennington Battle Monument shares eminence with nearby mountains. For the best view in town, visitors ride to an observation deck in the impressive 306-foot tower that commemorates a critical victory in the American Revolution. Regrettably, hikers don't have a similar option for getting uphill.

Plunked within walking distance of a city at the edge of a mountain range,

The historic Bennington Battle Monument, focal point of nearby hills.

"Bald" Mountain seems to promise great views in all directions, but thanks to a healthy growth of evergreens, the summit of this peak east of Bennington no longer lives up to its name. From its western end, the Bald Mountain Trail provides outlooks to greater Bennington and its column, but it's a rough path that can't compare to the pleasures of Harmon Hill (see Hike 2). I much prefer the other half, which begins in Woodford Hollow, climbs to open sky, and rewards hikers with eastern views of neighboring Green Mountain peaks.

Beginning at its eastern trailhead, the blue-blazed Bald Mountain Trail follows a driveway that swings into the woods and curls left behind a massive water tower. Crossing a brook within 150 yards, the route passes a cabin at the top of the first small ridge, and continues straight 40 yards later, where the jeep road bears to the left. Footing may be squishy along this narrow track, which occasionally shows signs of off-road vehicle use. Ignore old skid roads that periodically cross the trail, and keep a sharp eye on the blazes. Piled stones and a national forest boundary marker indicate a left turn onto a slender footpath 0.3 mile from the trailhead.

This cheery path weaves through sun-dappled woods of beech and paper birch, while brooks, rivulets, and assorted wet spots abound as you climb the gradual slope. A long, diagonal western vector soon carries the route up the steepest 0.25-mile pitch, until the trail rolls easily over the mountain's shoulder, curls northeast under cover of evergreens, and meets the path to Bear Wallow in an additional 0.2 mile. The Bear Wallow spur follows a level contour and supposedly finds a spring, but a long walk and produced nothing I'd drink on a recent exploration.

Four short switchbacks complete the 0.2-mile climb from the Bear Wallow spur to the junction with the West Ridge Trail, where fortunate hikers meet a dome of clear blue sky. Fast-growing evergreens belie the mountain's name, but a great alpine feeling persists on this breezy ridge and complements the day's best views of peaks to the east and south. Relax, have lunch, and pick out distant mountaintops before pushing on to the absolute summit, an easy 0.1-mile walk northeast on the West Ridge Trail.

Views are increasingly restricted at the top, but exploration should uncover Glastenbury, Equinox, and Dorset among the visible Green Mountain and Taconic Range peaks. If you're dead set on a western view, the Bennington outlook is a steep and ragged mile down the other side of the mountain. I prefer to return the way I came and hike to Harmon Hill.

4 HAYSTACK MOUNTAIN

General description:	A relaxing half-day family hike to a southern Green Mountain summit overlooking Haystack Pond.
General location:	Off Vermont Highway 9 about midway between Brattleboro and Bennington.
Length:	4 miles round-trip.
Difficulty:	Moderate.
Elevation gain:	1,000 feet.
Special attractions:	Easy access to four-state views of faraway peaks and sparkling waters. Optional walk to the wooded shore of a mountain pond.
Maps:	USGS Mount Snow quad.
For more information:	Manchester Ranger District, Routes 11 and 30, RR 1, Box 1940, Manchester Center, VT 05255; (802) 362-2307.

Finding the trailhead: From the junction of Vermont Highways 9 and 100 North in the center of Wilmington village, travel west on VT 9, 1.1 miles to a right (north) turn onto Haystack Road, at a sign for the Chimney Hill development. Proceed north on Haystack Rd. 1.2 miles, and turn left (west) onto paved Chimney Hill Road just as the road straight ahead turns to gravel.

The route weaves through a large development of vacation homes. After 0.2 mile, turn right at the top of a hill onto gravel Binney Brook Road. Stay left on Binney Brook Rd. at a fork after 0.1 mile, passing several turns for smaller streets until you reach a T at Upper Dam Road. Turn right at the T, left again in 0.1 mile, and you'll find a well-marked trailhead on your right in a final 0.15 mile. Park off the side of the road without blocking any driveways.

The hike: A simple jaunt to a modest summit, the Haystack Mountain Trail owes much to a Nordic tradition. Ensconced near a hub of winter recreation, this gradual route is designed to transport cross-country skiers from the open woods of a shallow ravine to a mountainous ridge that stretches to Mount Snow. In warmer months, the trail doubles as a great family hike, quickly trading its ski resort flavor for the freshness of a hardwood forest and excellent summit views.

The trail leaves a neighborhood of vacation homes on a wide, crushed stone track that angles slowly uphill, enters the Green Mountain National Forest, and meets a locked vehicular gate within only 200 yards. Marked with blue diamonds to guide intermediate skiers, the track slabs steadily upward following the small Binney Brook ravine below Haystack Mountain's elongated southern ridge. Slowly, the easily walked path converges with the flow of the stream, until the route departs from the jeep track, turning left onto a woodland path marked as the Haystack Mountain Trail less than 0.5 mile from the trailhead and only 20 yards after crossing the brook.

Slanting southward away from the summit, the forest path continues to ease above the brook for 0.2 mile before it veers sharply right (northwest) at a turn plainly marked by the orange diamond of a snowmobile route. Now climbing on an opposite tack, the trail gradually rises through beech-sprinkled woods and gains the top of the ridge where early and late season hikers catch glimpses of the summit ahead. A relaxed stroll through brambles that closely hug the trail leads to the narrow confines of an upper ridge and year-round views of Haystack's peak. Just when you feel that you're skirting too far beyond the western flank, a sign deflects hikers toward the summit, turning right (east) off a grassy path that continues to Mount Snow.

Blue ski markers persist beyond the final turn, but a few tight corners and rapid gains in elevation make the last 0.2 mile more suitable as a summer jaunt. Don't be upset when your mild exertion tops out on a rocky knoll surrounded by trees that severely limit the view. Instead, meander about 30 yards east on a web of brushy paths to a broad boulder outcrop, your ultimate destination.

Nestled close below the summit's evergreen-covered slopes, Haystack Pond commands your immediate attention, a natural barrier to the condos and chairlift towers that line the ski runs on Mount Snow. Sit a spell. Leisurely contemplation reveals remarkable four-state views. To the south, Vermont's Harriman Reservoir points a sparkling finger at distant Massachusetts summits, dominated by Mount Greylock rising above the crowd. To the west, New York's Adirondacks paint a sweeping backdrop for nearby Glastenbury Mountain circled by Green Mountain peaks. To the east, Mount Monadnock stands proudly in New Hampshire far beyond the Vermont hills that hide the Connecticut Valley.

An easy variant of this hike explores the source of Binney Brook. Rather than turning left on the woodland path, stay on the gravel jeep track. This route sustains a steady pace and leads to a Vermont Water Department cabin at the south end of Crystal Pond. Beyond the northwest corner of the cabin, a well-worn path skims past a public water supply and grants access to Haystack Pond. No camping, swimming, or picnicking is allowed within this area, but nothing prevents you from stretching your legs, breathing fresh air, and viewing Haystack Mountain above the western shore.

4 HAYSTACK MOUNTAIN

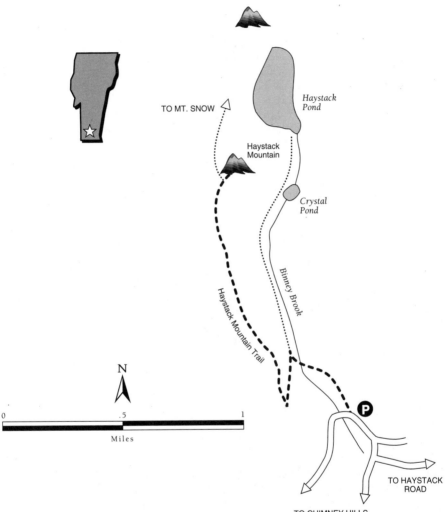

TO MT. SNOW

Haystack
Pond

Haystack
Mountain

Crystal
Pond

Binney Brook

Haystack Mountain Trail

N

0   .5   1

Miles

P

TO HAYSTACK
ROAD

TO CHIMNEY HILLS
DEVELOPMENT

5 LITTLE ROCK POND AND GREEN MOUNTAIN

General description:	An easy family backpack to campsites on Little Rock Pond, or a looping, scenic day hike that adds the Green Mountain summit.
General location:	About midway between Rutland and Manchester Depot.
Length:	4 miles round-trip to the pond; 6.8 miles for the Green Mountain loop.
Difficulty:	Moderate.
Elevation gain:	300 feet to the pond; 1,000 feet to the Green Mountain summit.
Special attractions:	Little Rock Pond, Green Mountain views, and camping at waterfront sites.
Maps:	USGS Danby and Wallingford quads.
For more information:	Manchester Ranger District, Routes 11 and 30, RR 1, Box 1940, Manchester Center, VT 05255; (802) 362-2307.

Finding the trailhead: Forest Road 10 runs east from U.S. Highway 7 about halfway between Rutland and Manchester Depot. Look for a paved four-way intersection near a hardware store where signs point west toward Danby and east toward Mount Tabor. Turn east in the direction of Mount Tabor, cross the railroad tracks, and enter the White Rocks National Recreation Area at Silver Bridge 0.9 mile from the highway. The parking lot for the northbound Long Trail/Appalachian Trail is on the right, 2.1 miles from Silver Bridge. The trailhead is across the road.

The hike: Located in the beautiful White Rocks National Recreation Area (part of Green Mountain National Forest) the scenic stretch of the Long Trail/Appalachian Trail (LT/AT) from Forest Road 10 to Little Rock Pond has earned a reputation as the perfect backpack for beginners. Two tenting areas, tent platforms, designated campsites, toilet facilities, ample water, and a caretaker on seasonal duty add to its credentials as a user-friendly destination. Throw in a sparkling lake and the optional climb to the views from the top of Green Mountain and you've assembled all the ingredients of an outstanding family hike.

Befitting a novice hike, the popular 2-mile walk from trailhead to pond is fairly level. From the end of the roadway bridge that spans Big Black Brook, hike north on the LT/AT following the west bank of the stream for only 50 yards. As the brook peels away to the right, the path skips to the top of the bank, wanders another 100 yards, and grazes an oxbow in the stream before the Big Black departs for good.

Shaded by tall stems of assorted deciduous trees, an easy saunter along the grade of a former logging road guides the trail 0.6 mile to a crossing of Little Black Brook on a narrow iron girder. Recrossing the same stream in

5 LITTLE ROCK POND AND GREEN MOUNTAIN

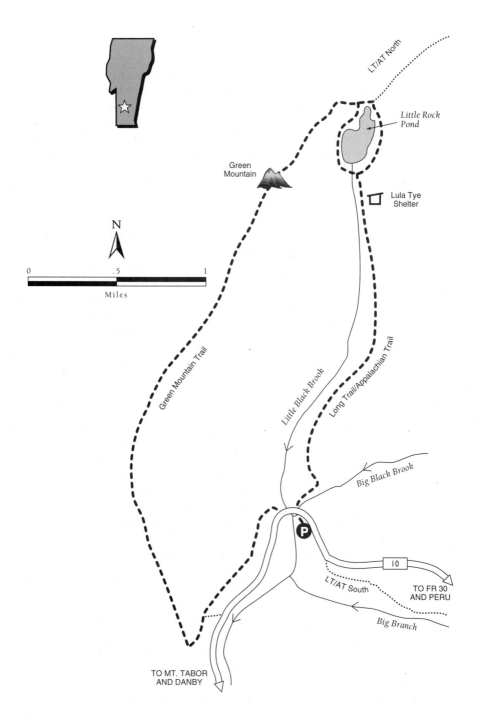

LT/AT North

Little Rock
Pond

Green
Mountain

Lula Tye
Shelter

N

0   .5   1

Miles

Green Mountain Trail

Little Black Brook

Long Trail/Appalachian Trail

Big Black Brook

P

10

LT/AT South

TO FR 30
AND PERU

Big Branch

TO MT. TABOR
AND DANBY

0.2 mile, the stroll resumes by hugging the brook on the damp ground east of the flow and spanning several marshy spots on walkways and well-placed stones. Mosquitoes love this place. Don't forget bug dope in spring.

In time, the trail narrows to a rocky path that slithers up the side of a hill and passes the Lula Tye Shelter, an open Adirondack-style lean-to only 0.2 mile from your goal. Declining gradually beyond the shelter to the southeast corner of Little Rock Pond, the trail pauses at the edge of the water where you'll find a directory map. To the left a trail circles south and then edges the western shore; on a somewhat rougher route that reconnects with the LT/AT at the northeast corner of the pond. To the right, the LT/AT eases past campsites on the eastern shore and steps into waterfront clearings with views of Green Mountain ledges plunging to the opposite bank. From the marshy southern inlet to a large, sunny boulder lapped by the western shore to a bridge that spans the outlet brook from a cove in the wild north end, there's plenty to explore at Little Rock Pond before gathering the family at a campsite around an evening fire.

Whether a short excursion from base camp or return leg of a day hike loop, the Green Mountain Trail presents an adventurous option. Departing the northwest corner of the pond about 200 yards south of the outlet bridge at the top of a 25-foot bank, this path rapidly finds the Green Mountain spine and climbs a moderate pitch as wispy views of the Vermont Valley tease hikers to the west. Approaching the midpoint of the day hike circle, the route scampers along a backbone of bare bedrock in the company of scented spruce, as it enters a section of trail that some may find confusing. Remember that double blazes are meant to signal a sudden turn and that many alternate paths in this area end with obstructed views.

Scrambling upward near the peak, you'll sense that the trail is about to descend when a set of double blazes marks another hasty turn. To the left, a well-worn spur veers across slabs of ledge on a sunny detour that's also scored with blazes. Have faith! Sooner or later you'll find the scenic outcrop views that are a highlight of the hike. Overlooking the southern half of Little Rock Pond, an eastern vista scans the tops of arching mountains and draws your gaze down the rambling valley that funnels Little Black Brook back to a ragged notch near the trailhead.

Descending south from the summit, the trail crosses to the western slope for a woodsy excursion that rolls in and out of a shallow col. After passing a spur on the left that sneaks a last look at the eastern views, the simple path drifts steadily down the mountain's southwestern flank until gaining momentum for a rapid slide down a wildly tilted midhill slope. Easing again, the trail ranges generally south, keeping pace with the slow decline of the Green Mountain ridge and tracking for more than a mile the patient course of an old woods road sharply graded into the pitch.

A small gap in the forest cover grants constricted views of Vermont Highway 7 and Dorset Peak as the path nears the most southerly point of the hike and then curls left to crest the ridge. Dropping away from towering hemlocks into a hardwood forest, the trail meets a discreet sign that points ahead to a picnic area on the nearby access road. Turn left here instead and walk uphill on a less-established trail that angles 0.6 mile north and ends at FR 10 just 100 yards west of the spot where you began.

6 BIG BRANCH BROOK, GRIFFITH LAKE, AND BAKER PEAK

General description:	A two- or three-day backpack circuit through the heart of the Big Branch Wilderness; a full day for stronger hikers.
General location:	Midway between Rutland and Manchester Depot.
Length:	13.4 miles.
Difficulty:	Intermediate.
Elevation gain:	1,400 feet.
Special attractions:	Griffith Lake, views from Baker Peak, and campsites in a vanished town.
Maps:	USGS Danby quad.
For more information:	Manchester Ranger District, Routes 11 and 30, RR 1, Box 1940, Manchester Center, VT 05255; (802) 362-2307.

Finding the trailhead: Follow the directions for Hike 5 (Little Rock Pond and Green Mountain). Trailhead parking for the Long Trail/Appalachian Trail south is just 0.15 mile farther east on Forest Road 10.

The hike: Roaring brook, pristine lake, vanished town, or scenic mountainside, whatever your pleasure, this extended loop through the Big Branch Wilderness delivers a zesty mix of superior camping options. Forest roads and side trails admit day trippers to parts of this varied circuit, but a few days of relaxed roaming with a pack strapped to your back is the way to discover the subtle charms of this delightfully diverse terrain.

The adventure begins downhill, as the Long Trail/Appalachian Trail (LT/AT) drops south away from Forest Road 10 with the sounds of Big Branch Brook rushing in your ears. Quickly entering the Big Branch Wilderness, the trail descends to a level bank comfortably above the potent stream where a log lean-to shelter waits 0.2 mile from the road. In the next 0.1 mile the path skims just high enough above the river for unfettered views into riffles and pools before a right turn over a suspension bridge carries the trail briskly to the opposite shore. Take a few minutes to rock hop into the middle of the scenic flow, then turn left and follow the defined path that continues to trek upstream.

Another short jaunt guides hikers to a junction with the Old Job Trail, the route of your return. Up to this point, the indirect course of your walk has merely evaded a tough river crossing. Now with rocks and roots slowing the journey, the LT/AT turns right 3.5 miles from Baker Peak, forsaking the Big Branch valley for an easy incline aimed at the mountaintop. Soon bending more directly south, the trail opens into a broad ramp that scampers through the hardwood forest and passes a detour to the Lost Pond Shelter about halfway between FR 10 and Baker Peak.

Entering a clearing south of the shelter, the trail joins an overgrown logging road, crosses a large culvert, and begins a slow curve to the right. Quickly veering left to re-enter the woods, the path then scrambles up a ragged slope before regaining a steady pace on a curiously gradual climb. It's not vegetation over your head but geology beneath your feet that hints of elevation gain as stratified rocks, shards of shale, and tips of thrusting boulders invade the trail that sneaks up on Baker Peak.

A modest climb of a ridgetop knoll and descent down the other side make you worry that you've lost the way, but persevere. An easy effort on slanted rock soon makes the peak feel undeserved. From Manchester to Wallingford, the noble scope of the Vermont Valley greets hikers on this glorious summit. A quarry on Dorset Peak sits directly across the way, Killington and Equinox mountains emerge to the north and south, and the stately Adirondacks line the western sky.

The LT/AT follows the top of a thrust line south from Baker Peak, 200 yards of angled slabs and iffy footing that can be avoided on a summit bypass in the event of bad weather. Just as the main route re-enters the woods,

Dorset Peak, US 7, and the Vermont Valley from the summit of Baker Peak.

6   BIG BRANCH BROOK, GRIFFITH LAKE, AND BAKER PEAK

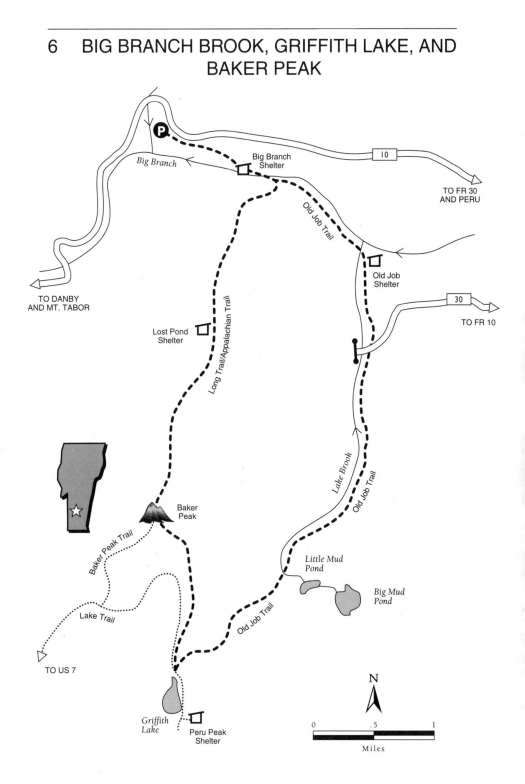

the Baker Peak Trail descends right toward U.S. Highway 7, while the LT bears left 1.8 miles from Griffith Lake on an easygoing path with brief descents that help you escape the heights.

Both the Lake Trail from the west and the Old Job Trail from the east intercept the LT/AT near the north end of Griffith Lake. This perfectly secluded backcountry pond serves as a turnaround point for the hike, a soothing place where day hikers may wish they could linger. A boardwalk conveys the LT/AT through evergreens on the eastern shore, guiding overnight guests to campsites near the water or toward the Peru Peak shelter 0.4 mile farther south. Keep in mind that camping is prohibited within 200 feet of Griffith Lake, except at designated sites.

The Old Job Trail is an optional route that returns hikers to the trailhead, an easy alternative that gobbles up miles as it churns along forest lanes. It also springs a few surprises. Running northeast from the end of Griffith Lake, a blue-blazed track coincides with a logging grade as it begins the 4.3-mile journey. Bear right when the trail meets the apex of a four-wheel-drive course, cross a bridge over the outlet of Little Mud Pond, and turn left following the flow of Lake Brook as it exits the watershed. While hikers parallel the eastern bank, cascades tumble through a deep ravine, small bridges span tributaries, and a forest road enters from the right. Stick with the wagon-track lane that continues downstream to the end of Forest Road 30 where a popular drive-in campsite hunkers beside the road.

Running north with the stream from FR 30, the Old Job Trail reverts to a pleasant path that connects to the Old Job Shelter. This log lean-to occupies a lovely clearing where a town blossomed in the 1880s as home to thirty families and thirty-five charcoal kilns. Take care as you cross the bouncing bridge near the left-hand corner of the shelter and enter the center of the vanished town, an extended clearing where swaying grass and goldenrod long since engulfed the apple trees. The startling remains of a sawdust pile form a moonscape on the right as the trail tramps the length of an obscure meadow, slides between spare trees, and trips over old kiln bricks. Tracing a grass-covered railroad grade, your wilderness loop comes to a quirky end as the trail sweeps the south bank of Big Branch Brook and reunites with the LT/AT just above the scenic suspension bridge 1.4 miles from the trailhead.

7   LYE BROOK WILDERNESS

General description:	An overnight backpack to a wilderness pond, or a half-day hike to a plummeting falls.
General location:	Between Bennington and Rutland, just east of Manchester Center.
Length:	14.6 miles round-trip.
Difficulty:	Intermediate.
Elevation gain:	1,900 feet.
Special attractions:	Wildlife, wetlands, Bourn Pond, and Lye Brook Falls.
Maps:	USGS Manchester, Sunderland, and Stratton Mountain quads.
For more information:	Manchester Ranger District, Routes 11 and 30, RR 1, Box 1940, Manchester Center, VT 05255; (802) 362-2307.

Finding the trailhead: About 0.4 mile east of U.S. Highway 7 on Vermont Highways 11 and 30, turn east onto East Manchester Road, proceed 1.1 mile, and then turn left onto Glen Road. Continue straight at the first fork onto a dead-end gravel road that leads to the trailhead in 0.4 mile.

The hike: Overshadowed by the height of Stratton Mountain and the fame of Stratton Pond (see Hike 1), this unheralded route through the heart of the Lye Brook Wilderness is a backcountry hiker's delight. Remote wetlands, a plummeting falls, and shelter near an unspoiled pond add luster to this rambling hike, which ends less than 3 miles from more popular haunts on the Long Trail (LT) corridor.

Day hikers on their way to Lye Brook Falls join the early procession as the Lye Brook Trail skirts the right side of a brushy clearing, aims at the sound of the brook, and bears left through a gauntlet of stones. Pausing for a quick look into the stream's ravine, the path joins the raised grade of an old logging railroad that tunnels straight through the pine-birch woods to a sign at the wilderness boundary. Lye Brook becomes a memory on the right while the trail reverts to a woodland road, rambles easily up a minimal slope, and discovers the awesome power of nature. In the summer of 1995, cyclonic winds ripped through this constricted valley, toppling hundreds of old-growth trees. As the road pitches up a moderate slope, hikers scramble over, under, around, and through the broken frameworks of the storm's victims.

Climbing steadily to merge with another railroad bed carved into the western slope, the trail jumps several sidehill streams and reaches a spur to the scenic falls 1.8 miles from the trailhead. Bear right for a 0.5-mile detour that traces a level contour and intercepts one of Vermont's most beguiling falls, a sinewy stream that plummets over towering strata of rock. Be cautious on the ledges overlooking this splendid diversion that you really shouldn't miss.

7 LYE BROOK WILDERNESS

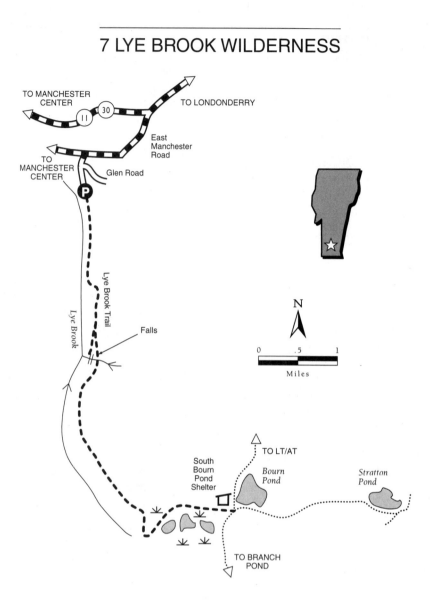

As the route ventures beyond the spur path to the falls and resumes its presistent climb, maple saplings and baby hemlocks suggest that this trail is little-used. Spanning the stream that feeds the falls, the trail slows to a measured pace and crosses a second brook after the bulk of the trek's elevation already has been gained. Mesmerizing acres of rock and wood set hikers' minds to musing in the course of the next 3 miles. Lost in thought, you may not notice as the trail evolves into a winding path deep in the autumn forest, a colorful carpet of fallen leaves caught between emerald ferns that cap a broad plateau.

After topping a tapered ridge, the trail evades a wetland, crosses a shaded

A sparkling welcome to the Lye Brook Wilderness.

bog and bends east past a chain of untamed marshes and silent beaver ponds. Here, in a rolling land of water and woods, Lye Brook makes good on its backcountry promise as wildlife and abundant campsites mingle beside the trail. If you need a more established site, bump through the woods for a solid 0.5 mile and drop into a comfortable lean-to that's hunkered beneath maples overlooking the south corner of Bourn Pond.

Happily settled in this elevated region of undulating terrain, backpackers are confronted with miles of agreeable options. Just over the bank between pond and shelter, Branch Pond Trail runs north past views of Stratton Mountain and marshes on a wilderness shore, eventually reaching a tenting area after 0.5 mile and a distant shelter near the LT junction a little south of Prospect Rock (see Hike 8). Turning south, the Branch Pond Trail crosses a brook within 40 yards and meets the 2.4-mile path leading to the LT at Stratton Pond (marked as the Stratton Pond Trail, but also known as an extension of the Lye Brook Trail). Linked together, this 10.7-mile triangulation of paths roves a pondside circuit that hosts days of carefree hiking with convenient frolics to views from Prospect Rock or Stratton Mountain and several of the prettiest campsites in all of southern Vermont.

8 PROSPECT ROCK, MANCHESTER

General description:	A convenient 3-hour excursion to an overlook at the edge of the Lye Brook Wilderness.
General location:	Southwestern Vermont, about 1 mile east of Manchester Depot.
Length:	3 miles round-trip.
Difficulty:	Moderate.
Elevation gain:	1,000 feet.
Special attractions:	Classic views of Mount Equinox, Manchester Center, and the picturesque Vermont Valley; early season access.
Maps:	USGS Manchester quad.
For more information:	Manchester Ranger District, Routes 11 and 30, RR 1, Box 1940, Manchester Center, VT 05255; (802) 362-2307.

Finding the trailhead: From the junction of U.S. Highway 7 and Vermont Highways 11 and 30, about 1 mile east of Manchester Depot, continue northeasterly on VT 11 East and VT 30 South 0.4 mile to the top of the first hill. Turn sharply right onto East Manchester Road then immediately left onto the gravel Rootville Road, which converges virtually at the same intersection. In 0.5 mile, the drivable portion of the road ends at the trailhead turnaround, just beyond a water tower. Parking is extremely limited, with the most logical area posted as a tow-away zone. Park off the road away from

8 PROSPECT ROCK, MANCHESTER

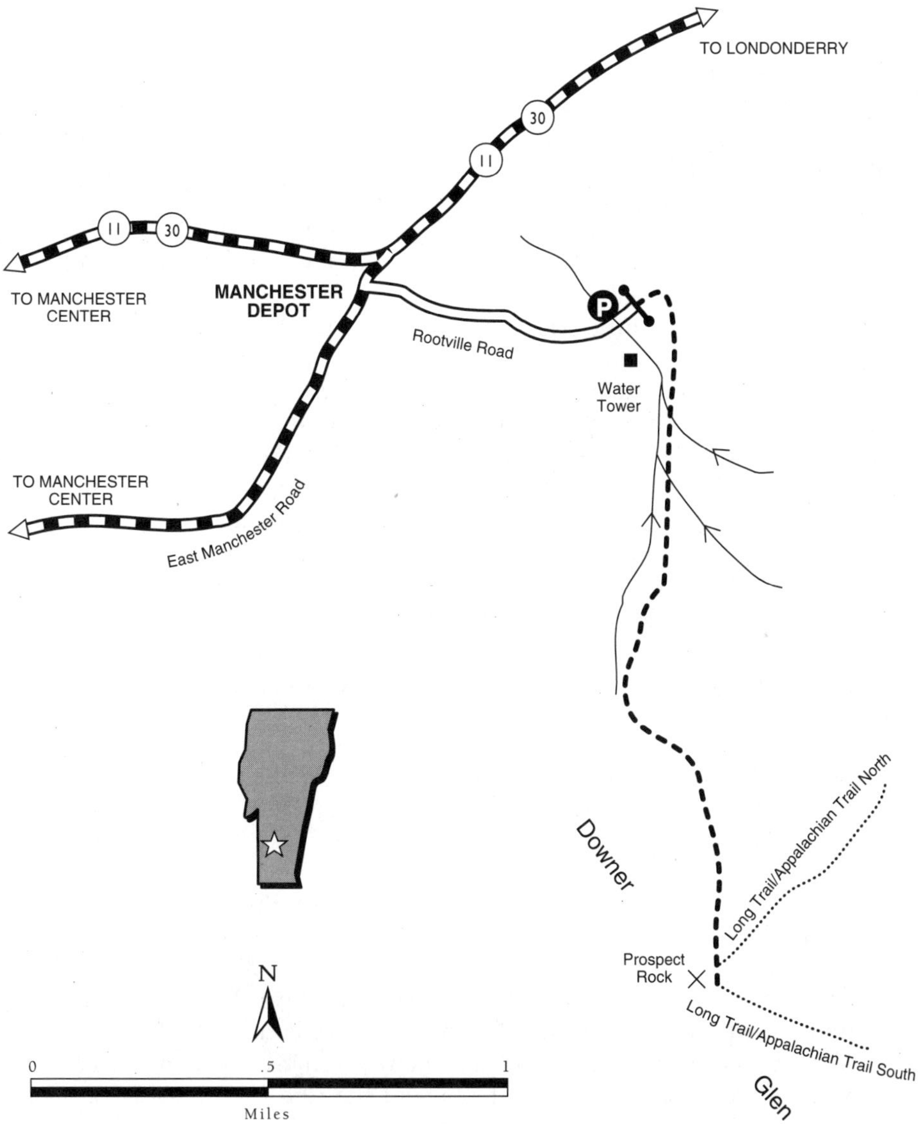

TO LONDONDERRY

30

11

11 30

TO MANCHESTER
CENTER

**MANCHESTER
DEPOT**

Rootville Road

TO MANCHESTER
CENTER

East Manchester Road

P

Water
Tower

Downer

Long Trail/Appalachian Trail North

Prospect
Rock ✕

Long Trail/Appalachian Trail South

Glen

N

0   .5   1
Miles

signs and driveways. If necessary, retreat down the road a bit to find a spot for your car.

The hike: Brand names such as Orvis and Timberland attract even hard-core hikers to the upscale shops and factory outlets that populate Manchester Depot. But when active visitors have had enough, a quick ramble to

Prospect Rock affords a welcome antidote to a day of rigorous browsing—or a very convenient diversion while companions shop 'til they drop. This walk along an old town road also serves as a perfect hike in the early spring to tune up unused muscles without eroding a muddy trail.

The old town road narrows as it curls above a water tower to the official Rootville trailhead. Entering Green Mountain National Forest, the track shrinks yet again, climbs moderately, and soon passes a small cascade sluices over slick rock on your right. Maple, ash, beech, and oak predominate as the road crosses a branch of the brook, keeps to the left (east) of the main channel, and scoots up the bottom of its own miniature valley. After crossing the primary stream on a wooden culvert, the slope naturally eases near the top of the watershed where staccato raps of a woodpecker may replace the sound of rushing water.

A hard left turn a little past the halfway point of the climb guides the road more directly upslope, angling toward the top of a steep ridge, which still remains unseen. Keep right with the main road where a smaller track departs to the left, directly opposite the first sign that marks the boundary of the Lye Brook Wilderness (see Hike 7). Within the next 200 yards the grade eases again as the road enters a cutbank section dissecting the side of the hill, opening views of the sparse flanks of Mount Equinox and the gleam of a Manchester steeple beyond the slopes of Downer Glen.

Safety netting prevents a disastrous descent off the edge of the graded road that now sweeps south parallel to the scenic ridge. With partridge bursting from cover, deer tracks under your feet, and beautiful vistas at your side, it's easy to miss the short spur path that leads to Prospect Rock. Look for stone steps that carry the Long Trail (LT) to the left (northeast), the double blazes of a trail intersection, and a series of narrow dirt paths to an outlook hidden behind trees 50 yards to your right. The first spur is located within 30 feet of the trail junction. If you find yourself hiking along a white-blazed track, you're headed south on the LT and have already missed the turn.

A United States Geological Survey benchmark fixes Prospect Rock at 2,079 feet, but hikers scurry a few feet higher to appreciate the excellent view. Past a corner of the Lye Brook Wilderness and the mouth of Downer Glen, the mountain-rimmed Vermont Valley sweeps northward from Manchester Center toward Danby, Wallingford, and Dorset and Peru peaks. It's a typical slice of the glacial valley that separates the western Taconic Range from the eastern slope of the Green Mountains, and the fine view makes you feel almost close enough to Manchester Depot to wave hello to your shopping friends.

9 WHITE ROCKS NATIONAL RECREATION AREA, ICE BEDS TRAIL

General description:	A short family walk from a picnic ground to mountain views and a really cool rock slide.
General location:	East of Wallingford, about 11 miles south of Rutland.
Length:	0.4 mile round-trip to the viewpoint; 1.9 miles round-trip to the ice beds.
Difficulty:	Moderate, but a slow, easy pace gets almost anyone to the viewpoint.
Elevation gain:	200 feet to the outlook; 500 feet round-trip to the ice beds.
Special attractions:	Unique views of White Rocks Cliff, potential falcon sightings, and an optional walk to cooling beds of ice.
Maps:	USGS Wallingford quad.
For more information:	Manchester Ranger District, Routes 11 and 30, RR 1, Box 1940, Manchester Center, VT 05255; (802) 362-2307.

Finding the trailhead: From the junction of U.S. Highway 7 and Vermont Highway 140 in Wallingford, follow VT 140 (School Street) 2.1 miles east and turn right at a fork marked with a sign for the White Rocks Recreation

White Rocks Mountain and boulder slides from sunny outcrops on the Ice Beds Trail.

9 WHITE ROCKS NATIONALRECREATION AREA, ICE BEDS TRAIL

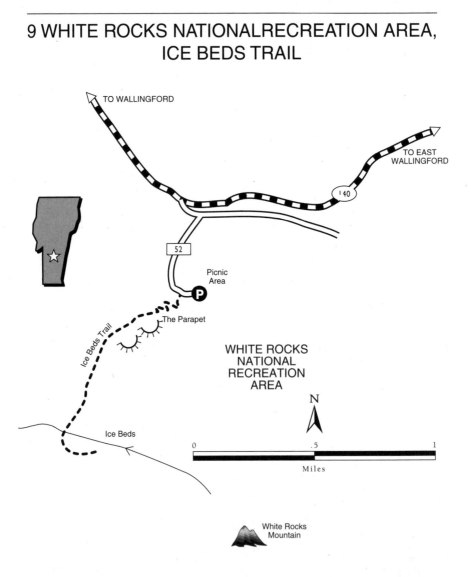

Area. Pass a single house and turn right again within 0.1 mile onto Forest Road 52 at another sign for a Green Mountain National Forest picnic area. The picnic grounds and parking lot are 0.5 mile down the road.

The hike: Sooner or later every hiker wakes up to a day when a nice picnic and an effortless walk to a nice view sounds like more than enough to do. On those rare occasions when hiking ambitions flag, White Rocks National Recreation Area faithfully answers the call. A broad lawn with picnic tables, a short path to unusual views, and large boulders basking in the sun all do their part to pleasantly prod the inertia of a lazy day. The Keewaydin Trail also leaves the White Rocks picnic area, but that's a vigorous connector to the Long Trail (LT) you can save for another day.

The Ice Beds Trail heads south from the near end of the parking lot and quickly crosses a wooden walkway that spans a tiny brook. Weaving through dense woods for a short distance, the path meets the bottom of a huge rockpile that forms a bony ridge and curls up the back of the jumble for several yards before bearing right and sidling up the stony slope. Five rapid switchbacks complete the first 0.1 mile as the trail carries hikers to directional signs at the top of the initial mound. A worthwhile diversion lies 50 yards to the left of the signs, where an outlook known as the Parapet regards the profile of White Rocks Cliff.

Starting the second half of the journey, the trail mounts the rocky spine again, swings right, and begins a slight descent. Several worn spur paths lead to pleasant overlooks on the left, but your real goal will be obvious as soon as you arrive. Broad, flat outcroppings of rock, perfect for lounging in the sun, offer stark views of White Rocks Cliff and the massive boulder slides that once sheared from the top of the mountain. Peregrine falcons have been known to nest on those barren crags, commanding views of the Otter Creek Valley and Green Mountain and Taconic Range summits that enclose vistas to the south.

At the base of one of those gigantic slides, winter snows pack into crevices between colossal boulders, making ice beds that cool the air and drip meltwater all summer long. Energetic types can extend their effort beyond the outlook on a last 0.6 mile of trail that dead-ends at the base of the slide. Descend quickly through groves of hemlock and pine on the Ice Beds Trail dropping down the far side of the ridge. At the bottom of the hill, continue straight ahead as the trail merges with an old woods road that joins to span a brook. Beyond the crossing, bear left and curl past another wet spot to the naturally refrigerated nooks and crannies at the source of the water flow. Cool off before you return the way you came. You're in for a bit of a climb.

THE TACONIC RANGE

OVERVIEW

A band of irregular mountains slanting across the southwestern border of Vermont, the Taconic Range is often more closely associated with the neighboring state of New York. Stretching from the Champlain Lowlands to the Hudson Highlands and separated from the dominant Green Mountains by the slender Vermont Valley, the low summits and snug hollows of this unique sliver of the state have largely been overlooked as potential hiking terrain. Picturesque and stunningly attractive, this hill country region of small villages and sloping farms obligingly shelters the Merck Forest and

Farmland Center, an environmental education resource where family hikers have the chance to explore the rumpled folds of this classic New England domain.

All regions have their exceptions, and in the Taconics it's Mount Equinox. Long a destination of mountain travelers, Vermont's highest peak outside of the Green Mountains supports a challenging trail and adds a touch of alpine splendor to this low-key mountain range.

10   MOUNT EQUINOX, BURR AND BURTON TRAIL

General description:	A vigorous, 4- or 5-hour round-trip climb to the highest summit in the Taconic Range.
General location:	Southwestern Vermont, immediately west of the village of Manchester.
Length:	6.8 miles round-trip, including Lookout Rock.
Difficulty:	Intermediate.
Elevation gain:	2,900 feet.
Special attractions:	Wildflowers, four-state views, and a marble bench overlooking the Vermont Valley.
Maps:	USGS Manchester quad.
For more information:	None available.

Finding the trailhead: From the intersection of U.S. Highway 7 and Vermont Highways 11 and 30, follow VT 30 west 1.5 miles to its terminus at Vermont Highway 7A in Manchester Center. Turn left onto VT 7A, drive 1.2 miles south, and turn right onto Seminary Avenue as you enter Manchester village. Turn left onto Prospect Street directly in front of the Burr and Burton Seminary, then right onto West Union Street in another 0.2 mile. The first driveway on your right enters a large gravel parking area provided by the seminary. The trailhead is at the far left corner as you enter the lot.

Sky Line Drive, the toll road to the top of Mount Equinox, is off VT 7A 4.3 miles south of the right turn onto Seminary Ave.

The hike: Fly fishing the crystal clear Battenkill River, strolling the meadows of the Hildene Estate, or shopping its elegant streets, visitors find Manchester's aura strictly genteel. Few would guess that around back of the famous Equinox Inn a legitimately challenging mountain hike begins at the center of town. The Burr and Burton Trail climbs Mount Equinox, the precipitous mass that blocks the afternoon sun, the tallest summit in the Taconic Range rises more than 2,800 feet above the valley floor.

Unquestionably, Equinox is a mountain of contrasts. Although much of its land is protected by the Equinox Preservation Trust, the summit features a 1950s-style inn complete with the Bear Town Bar. While hikers labor to a

10 MOUNT EQUINOX, BURR AND BURTON TRAIL

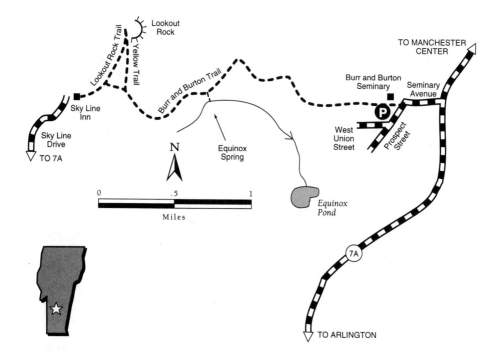

well-earned vista from secluded Lookout Point, tourists motor up the toll road to share the popular view. Your approach to this mountain, and your reaction to it, is purely a personal choice.

The hiking trail leaves the parking lot behind the Burr and Burton Seminary at a chained jeep track marked with blue blazes that edge west along an athletic field. After 100 yards, the path momentarily narrows and skims past private land before it meets a bright red gate at the end of an access road. Here a large sign explains the Equinox Preservation Trust and makes it clear that this entrance gate should not be used as a drive-in trailhead.

About 20 yards beyond the red gate, a trail sign points the way to the summit along a well-maintained dirt road. Bear right at a V in another 0.15 mile where a third sign points left to a pond. The route soon skirts a cabin clearing as it eases and curls toward the ominous flanks of Mount Equinox flickering through the trees ahead. Wildflowers distract hikers from their efforts on these sunny slopes, where springtime violets and trillium bloom before the hatch of the first black flies.

As the path nears the base of the vertical pitch, the gravel track begins an unrelenting ascent that veers southwest 1 mile from the trailhead, with no slack in pace. Bromley Mountain and Downers Glen rise into view across the valley, while the hearty climb continues to a small cairn that announces a detour to Equinox Spring (200 feet ahead) and a right turn onto the narrow continuing path. The smaller path is no less steep. The aerobic challenge persists.

Loggers apparently never made it to these heights. Giant specimens of birch and beech line the airy trail, give sustenance to abundant grouse, and impart a less civilized feel. As the Vermont Valley unfolds more lavishly with each ascending step, the trail jogs suddenly right 2,000 feet above the trailhead. With nearly a mile of mountain shoulder still left between you and summit, the heaviest going ends. Angling northwest, on generally friendlier slopes, the route soon intersects the red and yellow trails 0.2 mile from the top.

Confusion reigns near the summit. Red and yellow blazes lead off in two directions, while the blue-blazed Burr and Burton Trail continues straight ahead as a vague, overgrown path. Judging by trail conditions, most hikers bear right on the yellow trail for the 0.5-mile walk to Lookout Rock. No matter that this recommended route sports blazes in different colors, the easy path leads to a wood and marble bench overlooking the town with exquisite eastern views. From the small, barren outcrop, the Green Mountain peaks of Bromley and Stratton transcend the sprawling valley, while hints of Mount Monadnock and the White Mountains of New Hampshire peer faintly through the haze.

The wider Lookout Rock Trail parallels the yellow trail for a time as it returns along a wooded ridge bearing southwest toward the Equinox summit. This easy 0.5-mile stroll visits a memorial to a dog's untimely death and passes a transmission tower where the upper leg of the Burr and Burton Trail straggles to an end. A larger tower, Sky Line Inn, and a parking lot at the end of Sky Line Drive announce your arrival at the top.

Hikers mingle with auto passengers who amble about the summit enjoying the alpine scene. Although Lookout Rock still provides the best view to the north and east, a final ascent to the inn's second floor deck greatly enhances the outlook to the west and south. From this highest Equinox perch, the Adirondacks of New York, the Berkshires of Massachusetts, and the Taconic Range of Vermont radiate into the distance, concealing rivers and lowlands behind their countless peaks.

11 MERCK FOREST AND FARMLAND CENTER

General description: Day hikes or family backpacks through a community-supported environmental education center.

General location: Southwestern Vermont, about midway between Bennington and Rutland.

Length: 3.7-mile loop.

Difficulty: Easy to moderate.

Elevation gain: 400 feet.

Special attractions: Wildlife, views, wagon rides, farm animals, overnight shelters, and an old-fashioned swimming hole.

Maps: Handout maps are available at the visitor center or from the address below; also, USGS Pawlet quad.

For more information: Merck Forest and Farmland Center, Route 315, Rupert Mountain Road, P.O. Box 86, Rupert, VT 05768; (802) 394-7836.

Finding the trailhead: From Manchester Center, follow Vermont Highway 30, 8.1 miles north through the village of Dorset to the town of East Rupert. Turn left (west) onto Vermont Highway 315 and pass several attractive farms before reaching the sign for the Merck Forest and Farmland Center after 2.6 miles at the top of the hill. The gravel access road leads 0.5 mile to a parking area near the visitor center and trailhead.

The hike: If you'd like to teach kids about hiking, camping, respect for nature, or preservation of the environment, the Merck Forest and Farmland Center is an ideal place to start. About 28 miles of trails on more than 2,800 acres in the rolling hills of southwestern Vermont make this nonprofit center a terrific destination for all members of the family, but younger children eager to begin an outdoor education certainly will gain the most. With farm animals, wagon rides, overnight cabins, lean-to shelters, moderate trails, wildlife, glorious views, a sugar house, and swimming hole, there's not much here your basic kid won't enjoy.

Part of the charm of the Merck Center lies in its lack of pretense. First and foremost, this farm makes use of productive land that hikers are welcome to share. Cattle, sheep, ducks, and horses live in pastures near the trailhead, happy for handouts or a friendly pat, but without that artificial petting zoo air. Lean-tos and cabins are also sequestered along several trails, ready to shelter beginning hikers, but not at the expense of sugar bush and pastures needed for the farm. In the end, most families find these rolling hilltops to be trustworthy places to walk, explore, and expand their limits in a friendly atmosphere. For maps, camping reservations, program schedules, fees, or other information stop in at the visitor center or make contact at the above address.

The modest loop that passes Birch Pond and Spruce Mountain's viewpoint spur doesn't penetrate the far corners of this acreage, but it does take hikers past the busy barnyard to a few less traveled paths. From the gate near the visitor center, follow Old Town Road straight through a White Birch forest to a hillside meadow with long distance mountain views. Here, at the junction of Stonelot and Old Town roads, farm animals congregate in pastures near the barn, swallows perch on fences, and Spruce Mountain stares down at organic gardens from across the narrow valley. Stay right with Old Town Rd. as it dips into the hollow between the sheep and cattle pastures and rises easily along the edge of a clearing, lost in views stretching as far as the Adirondacks to the north and west.

After Gallup Road departs to the left, Old Town Rd. enters the woods, swings west to avoid Spruce Peak, and climbs steadily with bird calls filling the forest and a rooster's crows echoing up the valley. At the top of the hill, Antone Road departs to the right and Lodge Road (your likely route of return) enters through Spruce Clearing 30 yards later on the left. Now briefly cast as a two-wheel track, Old Town Rd. skims the edge of the upland meadow with views of Mount Equinox dead ahead and glimpses of Spruce Cabin on the far side of a clearing to the east. Easing in and out of the woods as it rambles down the southwestern flank of Spruce Mountain, the comfortable track follows sap tubing hitched to maple trees and hones in on the shrieks of splashing children on its approach to the swimming hole.

Old Town Road rolls through pastures at the Merck Forest and Farmland Center.

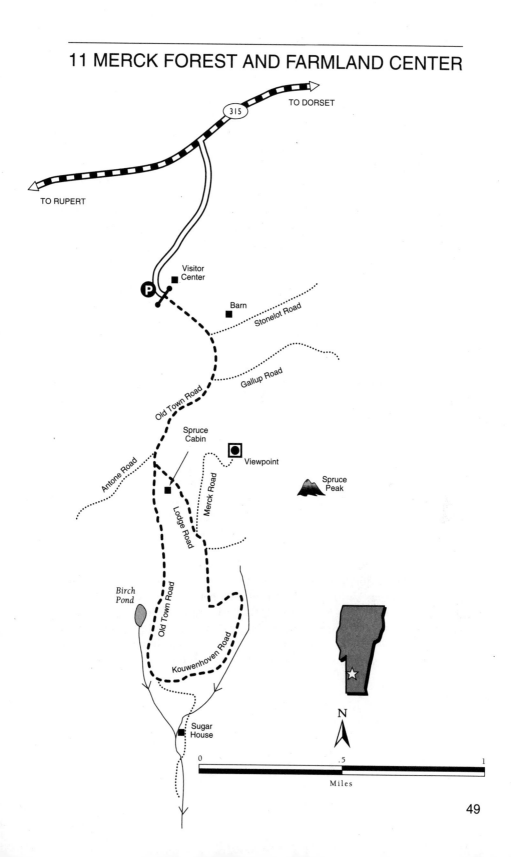

11 MERCK FOREST AND FARMLAND CENTER

315

TO DORSET

TO RUPERT

Visitor Center

P

Barn

Stonelot Road

Gallup Road

Old Town Road

Spruce Cabin

Viewpoint

Antone Road

Merck Road

Spruce Peak

Lodge Road

Birch Pond

Old Town Road

Kouwenhoven Road

Sugar House

N

0   .5   1

Miles

49

Summer or not, everyone enjoys Birch Pond, a scenic pool shadowed by woods, shared by beaver and plenty of fish. Remember, though, the risk is yours; no lifeguards are on duty. This watery diversion is a refreshing start to the second half of the hike, which curls through a lean-to dotted glade and then turns left onto Kouwenhoven Road for a definitive change of pace. Skirting the base of a hillside grove of birch, this grassy swath winds back to the top of the ridge accompanied only by songbirds and the murmur of a stream through a deep ravine.

Kouwenhoven Rd. bears left at a faint fork as it nudges close to the stream and turns sharply back on itself on a final slope. A long, flat walk through trees widely dispersed along the ridge eases hikers back to a second junction with Lodge Road. Turn left, pass Merck Road, and continue north through Spruce Clearing to complete a loop that returns to Old Town Rd. near its highest point.

For a different perspective, Merck Rd. diverges right and ascends diligently behind the staff quarters to a viewpoint knoll that holds benches and a fire ring. Along with distant mountains, this detour often reveals the gobble of a wild turkey or a barred owl's hoot on a cloudy day.

THE SOUTHERN UPLANDS

OVERVIEW

Squeezed between soaring Green Mountain peaks and the southern Connecticut Valley, the mixed topography of this slender region displays a mingled landscape as ambiguous as its name. A blend of rolling hills, gentle valleys, and isolated peaks typical of rural New England, these scenes frequently are bypassed by hikers who favor nearby landscapes more prominently supplied with mountains.

Of course, natural beauty isn't limited to the highest peaks. From the Massachusetts border to Interstate 89 the familiar contours of this earthy region sustain abundant attractions that generously reward those who are willing to seek them out. Amity Pond, Bald Mountain, Eshqua Bog, and the north side of Ludlow Mountain (what skiers call Okemo) provide peaceful walks, engaging views, and collections of plants and animals that naturally enrich Vermont's singular version of a backyard wilderness.

12 AMITY POND NATURAL AREA

General description:	A 2-hour walk through a peaceful preserve, with overnight shelters for hikers who wish to linger.
General location:	Central Vermont, about 10 miles north of Woodstock.
Length:	2 miles round-trip.
Difficulty:	Easy to moderate.
Elevation gain:	600 feet.
Special attractions:	Mountain views and natural solitude.
Maps:	Handout maps are available from the address below; also USGS Quechee and Woodstock North quads.
For more information:	Vermont Agency of Natural Resources, Department of Forests, Parks and Recreation, District I, RR 1, Box 33, North Springfield, VT 05150; (802) 886-2215.

Finding the trailhead: From the junction of U.S. Highway 4 and Vermont Highway 12 in Woodstock, follow VT 12 north across the Ottauquechee River. After 1.2 miles, turn right toward South Pomfret and the Suicide Six Ski Area at a fork where VT 12 branches left. Bear right at the post office and general store in South Pomfret and drive 4.7 miles to Hewetts Corners, an anonymous intersection where a left turn follows small signs pointing toward Sharon and Interstate 89. Continue only 0.2 mile then turn left again onto a gravel road that angles off the highway. After this turn, stay left at 1 mile, go right after 2 miles, and park off the road at the top of the hill 2.2 miles from the highway. Look closely. A trailhead sign is 15 yards into the woods behind a gap in a stone wall on the left.

The hike: Traveling to Amity Pond through valleys stocked with black-and-white cattle and maple syrup signs, visitors are prone to expect a romantic pool circled by lush wildflower meadows and stunning mountain views. Reality dashes such illusions. In fact, Amity Pond is a tiny kettle hole well disguised by brambles and poplar trees, so flagrantly unappealing that astute hikers will immediately suspect that there must be more to the story.

A gift to the people of Vermont from Elizabeth and Dick Brett, the Amity Pond Natural Area was meant to conserve an environment of solace and shelter, a refuge of peace and quiet, forever free from the sight, sound, and smell of intrusive modern machines. Their goal has been achieved. To be sure, these acres do contain a high pasture, distant view, and sparkling upland stream, but a mellow pace unfolds this preserve's less obvious delights. Log shelters for overnight guests, tiny pools under giant maples, and a deep and abiding silence focus attention on bobolinks that call in the meadow and turtles that make a delicate splash as you approach the namesake pond. Tarry here awhile and you will recall that the beauty of a natural area is never just skin deep.

Delicate beauty blankets the forest floor.

52

12 AMITY POND NATURAL AREA

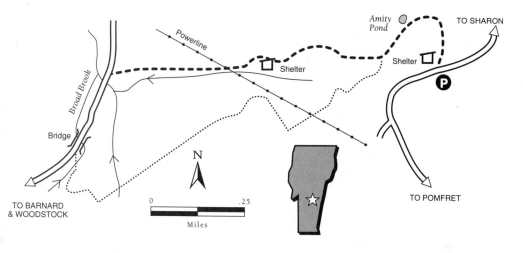

From a welcoming sign in a clearing a few paces off the road, a path to the left leads 80 yards to a lean-to shelter and fire ring overlooking a tiny pond. To the right, the main trail swings through a thicket and loops into a field invaded by brambles and transitional trees. Following a dirt track like a cattle path through a pasture, hikers pass invisible Amity Pond hidden behind a tangled screen 20 feet to the right, and top out 40 yards later on a small knoll with southwestern views to Mount Tom, the tip of Mount Ascutney, Killington, and Pico Peak.

When you descend south off the knoll, it's time to make a choice. Although a loop hike is possible, the southerly route on the path straight ahead may be more than you bargained for, a sometimes muddy, often steep descent more appropriate as a ski trail. For a simple nature walk, the northern route is more in keeping with the rest of the hike.

Both options bear older signs that read "Hawk's Hill & E. Barnard." To find the easier (northern) course, keep a sharp look out as you walk downhill three-quarters of the way from the knoll to the edge of the woods. A new sign for the Amity Pond Trail and the Sugar Arch Shelter points along a faint path to the right that rolls over a hump in the meadow and descends a shallow swale before conspicuously entering the woods.

Birdsong filters through maples as the path guides hikers down a gradual slope to a spacious mound splashed with violets spread beneath hardwood trees. Another descent through a forest of birch and beech soon leads to the Sugar Arch Shelter, where a barrel hoop around the trunk of a fair-sized tree reminds visitors of the region's agricultural past. Twirling through a small forest clearing to conclude the downhill hike, the route turns left onto an old logging road that ducks under a power line and nudges a gentle stream on its way to the top of a meadow. From the field/forest border a trampled path saunters through the grass, samples the shade of two apple trees, and savors a churchyard view on Broad Brook Road far across the field ahead.

Most visitors will want to relax in the quiet meadow and return the way they came, but for those compelled to complete a loop, the other prong of this hike meets Broad Brook Road just beyond a tiny bridge a few hundred yards to the left (south). The junction is marked with a brand-new sign, but the trail is a bit obscure. Loop walkers may find it easier to begin their hike by descending the southern route.

To begin a loop on the alternate (southerly) route from the top of the viewpoint knoll, continue straight to the edge of the woods, ignore a trail that heads left toward South Pomfret, and be prepared for a twisting downhill run. Nearing the bottom of the slope, the trail follows an old logging road for less than 100 yards before turning right, eventually crossing a stream, and zigzagging sharply to join a larger lane. Turn right parallel to Broad Brook until you see a modern gravel road. The trail jumps the stream at a difficult crossing about 20 yards south of a concrete bridge on Broad Brook Road. To link up with the western end of the northerly trail, turn right (north) on Broad Brook Road, pass two houses, and turn right onto a path of crumpled grass that aims between two apple trees on the upper end of the meadow. Trail signs resume at the edge of the woods.

13 BALD MOUNTAIN, TOWNSHEND

General description:	An elementary family hike from campground to summit in southern Vermont.
General location:	18 miles north of Brattleboro.
Length:	3.1 miles.
Difficulty:	Moderate.
Elevation gain:	1,100 feet.
Special attractions:	Covered bridge, campsites, a parklike summit, and southern mountain views.
Maps:	Handout maps are available at the campground or from the address below.
For more information:	Department of Forests, Parks and Recreation, District I, RR 1, Box 33, North Springfield, VT 05150; (802) 886-2215.

Finding the trailhead: From the junction of Vermont Highways 30 and 35 in Townshend, follow VT 30, 2 miles north and turn left onto a one-lane bridge over the spillway of the Townshend Reservoir dam. Drive straight through the first intersection beyond the dam, continue 0.2 mile to a T, and turn left onto a gravel road, following signs for Townshend State Park. Within 1.1 mile, the gravel road passes the Scott Covered Bridge and tracks the

13 BALD MOUNTAIN, TOWNSHEND

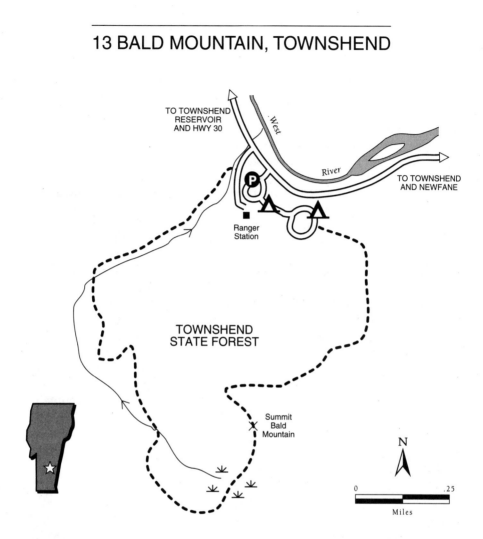

West River to the entrance of the park. Hikers will find parking on the right (west) side of the driveway just before the ranger station. Register and pay the small day-use fee. The trailhead is just beyond the parking area on the right.

The hike: Hidden between the Connecticut Valley and the Green Mountain National Forest, Bald Mountain and Townshend State Park quietly draw visitors to an unsung pocket of Vermont. Part of 856-acre Townshend State Forest, this diminutive summit and decidedly quirky trail add just the right measure of family adventure to an inviting destination. A unique summit, spacious campsites, a huge covered bridge, play areas, and a sandy beach a short way down the road (see Hike 15) guarantee all members of the family plenty of weekend fun.

Most people make a brief stop before arriving at the mountain. Only 0.5 mile from the entrance to Townshend State Park, Scott Covered Bridge stretches 276 feet across the shallow West River. Once the longest single span in Vermont, visitors can still walk through this wooden tunnel and marvel at the skill required to join its massive beams and fashion its arching trusses. Before you leave, be sure to read the speed limit sign posted at the end of the bridge.

To begin the well-marked 1.7-mile trail leading to the top of Bald Mountain, walk west from the ranger station, jog right on a campground road, and enter the woods near campsite 25. The route quickly crosses a tiny bridge, turns left on an old town road, and weaves upward following the channel of a boulder-strewn brook. Amusing markers soon begin to appear identifying basswood, elm, hemlock, and ash amidst the profusion of surrounding trees. Whimsical signs also register the trail's elevation gain, as hikers climb past 800 feet and cross to the opposite side of the stream.

Good footing and moderate grades spin the trail southeast on a long, looping approach to the far side of the peak, interrupted only by duff and protruding stones on switchbacks rising from 1,000 to 1,100 feet. After a short decline, a large glacial erratic touches the edge of the trail near two crossings of a smaller brook. The path then bends east, scampers over slabs, and clips the end of an alder swamp nearly 1,400 feet above sea level.

Ascending through sunny realms of grass, reclining boulders, and ancient specimens of well-spaced evergreen and oak, the last section of trail rises an additional 280 feet through parklike settings on Bald Mountain's

Scott Covered Bridge, once the longest single span in Vermont.

rounded top. This enticing expanse of airy summit encourages carefree wandering. Observant hikers can locate views of Mount Monadnock in New Hampshire to the east, and glimpses of Stratton and Bromley mountains farther west in southern Vermont.

Hikers who'd like to complete a loop can explore a much steeper, 1.4-mile alternative path that connects the summit of Bald Mountain to the eastern end of the camping area. Be careful though—the rough-hewn path becomes more difficult right away. Plunging through dense stands of conifers just below the peak, this optional course tightropes course down and across a north-facing slope where views of the Townshend Reservoir are sadly overgrown. The trail slowly regains reliable footing as it descends through a hemlock grove and saunters through hardwoods into the campground near campsite 21. Follow the camp road west toward the ranger station to make your way back to your car.

14   ESHQUA BOG NATURAL AREA

General description:	A short stroll over boardwalk and path through a wetland natural area.
General location:	Near Woodstock, about 11 miles west of White River Junction.
Length:	0.45-mile circuit.
Difficulty:	Easy.
Elevation gain:	From 0 to 50 feet, depending on chosen route.
Special attractions:	Rare wildflowers in an upland fen.
Maps:	Handout maps are available from the address below.
For more information:	The Nature Conservancy, 27 State Street, Montpelier, VT 05602; (802) 229-4425.

Finding the trailhead: From Interstate 89, Exit 1, follow U.S. Highway 4 west 10.4 miles to the outskirts of Woodstock village. At a gas station on a curve where US 4 turns right 90 degrees, turn left onto Hartland Hill Road. Proceed 1.2 miles and turn right onto Garvin Hill Road, the first gravel road on the right. After 1.3 miles look for a large trailhead sign in the woods on the right. A pullout accommodates two cars. Otherwise, park as best you can off the traveled portion of the road.

The hike: Hidden in the woods off a narrow dirt road on a hill southeast of town, Eshqua Bog is a wildflower lover's delight. Owned and managed by The Nature Conservancy and the New England Wild Flower Society, this compact 40-acre wetland site preserves an astounding array of botanical life, from marsh marigolds and common bunchberry to the beauty of rare orchids. Photographers, connoisseurs of native plants, and hikers who would

14 ESHQUA BOG NATURAL AREA

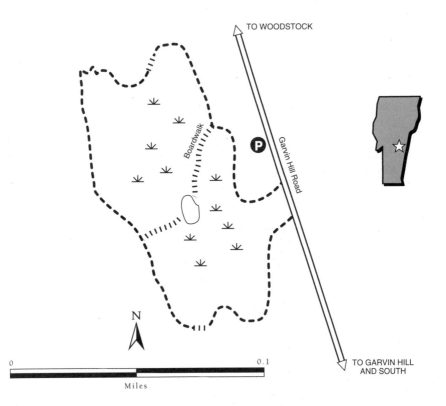

like to immerse themselves in nature's wild profusion are drawn to this fen teeming with species that harken back to post-glacial New England.

Don't expect the sparkle of open water to guide you to this site—first-time visitors may even wonder what happened to the bog. Only a large sign three strides into the forest differentiates the trailhead from miles of anonymous frontage on a wooded country road. Follow the white blazes of the spongy trail a few paces through the trees, though, and the path soon turns right (north) to skirt a fern-filled wetland glade. Passing over wooden planks where scouring rush and goldthread cover the damp woodland floor, the path reaches a registration box and a significant junction of trails.

Straight ahead, the route circles the bog's northern lobe under maples, poplar, and birch, crosses the outlet on a marigold-bordered bridge, scampers 50 feet up the opposite bank, and meanders down to meet the far end of the alternate path. Although Eshqua trails are short enough to allow exploration of them all, anyone requiring very easy footing should bypass this northern loop. Instead, turn left at the registration box and opt for the highlight of the day, a fascinating boardwalk that leads to an island at the center of the bog.

Stalking wildflowers at Eshqua Bog.

Identification signs pinpoint many species, but a wildflower guide would make a welcome addition to this fascinating trip. Bisecting an otherwise impenetrable bog, the boardwalk trail exposes ferns and mosses, swamp saxifrage, cattails, lady's slipper orchids, wild sarsaparilla, purple avens, pitcher plants, and hordes of other varieties that weave an incredibly profuse display. From dewy blossoms at your feet to lacy larch high in the upper story, jumbles of vegetation infuse the trail with the glory of nature's bounty. Watch for two plants in particular—exquisite yellow lady's slipper orchids that embody the ideal of fragile beauty, and clumps of poison ivy that enforce the warning to stay on the trail.

The boardwalk ends on the far (west) side of Eshqua Bog. Turn left to complete the loop around the southern end of the fen, as the trail edges just high enough to keep your boots dry above the wetland border. Crossing the inlet stream on a board bridge, the path curls gently through camouflaging forest and empties back onto the anonymous road about 30 yards south of the original trailhead.

15 LEDGES OVERLOOK TRAIL

General description:	A short recreational trail to an outcrop high above Townshend Lake.
General location:	18 miles north of Brattleboro.
Length:	1.7 miles.
Difficulty:	Moderate.
Elevation gain:	300 feet.
Special attractions:	Beach, picnic grounds, pavilion, and views of the West River valley.
Maps:	Trail maps are posted in the picnic area and may be available from the address below.
For more information:	U.S. Army Corps of Engineers, Townshend Lake, RR 1, Box 2800, Townshend, VT 05353; (802) 365-7703.

Finding the trailhead: From the junction of Vermont Highways 30 and 35 in Townshend, follow VT 30, 2 miles north and turn left onto a one-lane bridge over the spillway of the Townshend Reservoir dam. Enter the Townshend Lake Recreation Area by turning right onto a blacktop road at the first intersection beyond the dam. Park on the right 0.6 mile past the entrance. The trailhead is across the road.

The hike: Less than 2 miles from the entrance to Townshend State Park (see Hike 13), the recreational facilities at Townshend Lake add a dash of luxury to hiker options. Maintained by the U.S. Army Corps of Engineers, the sandy beach, pavilion shelters, and extensive picnic grounds rimming

15 LEDGES OVERLOOK TRAIL

the western shore indulge the passive pleasures of a steamy summer day. For a little exercise before firing up charcoal in the grill, the Ledges Overlook Hiking Trail supplies an aerobic workout by means of a brisk climb to a nearby outcrop with local views not available on Bald Mountain.

The simple loop begins by scooting directly up the hill across the road from a large pavilion. Beech and maple trees mix with a few large pines as the path converges with an old stone wall and soon swings left to gradually tackle the slope. Tracking south with solid footing that maintains an upward march, the path turns sharply right at the decrepit end of another wall, bears briefly west, and then turns sharply right again in line with a narrow ridge. The remains of several charred acres of underbrush remind hikers of the danger of fire in a section of trail that skims the crest of the ridge and pauses at the Ledges Overlook. Bald Mountain, Townshend Lake, an arching strip of beach, the earthen dam, and the winding West River Valley all contribute to a local view that's much better than you might expect.

Leaving the ledges, the path jumps to the top of a knoll, visits an ancient oak, and strolls through a woodland savannah occupying the ridge. This unusual stand of hop hornbeam scattered on a grassy lawn signals the beginning of a rapid descent through a constantly changing pattern of forest succession. The workout concludes by returning to the access road about 400 feet north of the point where you began. Turn right to find the trailhead.

16   OKEMO MOUNTAIN, HEALDVILLE TRAIL

General description:	A half-day climb on a little-known trail to remarkable fire tower views.
General location:	Near Ludlow, about 15 miles southeast of Rutland.
Length:	5.8 miles round-trip.
Difficulty:	Intermediate.
Elevation gain:	1,900 feet.
Special attractions:	Woodlands, wildflowers, and 360-degree fire tower views.
Maps:	USGS Ludlow and Mount Holly quads.
For more information:	Department of Forests, Parks and Recreation, District I, RR 1, Box 33, North Springfield, VT 05150; (802) 886-2215.

Finding the trailhead: Follow Vermont Highways 100 and 103 north from the middle of Ludlow past the entrance to Okemo Ski Area. Continue straight on VT 103 when VT 100 departs to the right 1.7 miles from the center of town. Turn left onto Station Road 2.7 miles later. The pavement ends before Station Rd. crosses railroad tracks 0.7 mile from VT 103. Turn left just across the tracks at a sign for Healdville Trail parking. As you make the final turn, you can see the small parking lot at the end of the road.

The hike: Mount Okemo rises only 15 miles due west of Mount Ascutney, but geological differences prove that these mountains originated half a world apart. A portion of the billion-year-old Precambrian Green Mountain core, Mount Okemo is native to these parts, carved by glaciers into soft contours that reach out to surrounding hills. Mount Ascutney, by contrast, is the new kid on the block, an ice-resistant chunk of White Mountain pluton that crossed the Atlantic only 350 million years ago to stand in stark isolation above a valley floor. In practical terms, the geological history of these neighboring summits explains why Mount Okemo supports a kinder, gentler trail.

USGS maps refer to this elongated mass as Ludlow Mountain, but a ski resort on the eastern slope and a state forest on the north lend Okemo its popular name. From the site of the former Healdville Station on the edge of Okemo State Forest, the blue-blazed Healdville Trail parallels still-active railroad tracks, crosses a brook, and curls right to begin a modest climb. Recently constructed by the Vermont Youth Conservation Corps, the new trail passes faint vestiges of several old logging roads as it spans a second stream on heavy beams and meanders upward, roughly following the course of a mossy brook.

16 OKEMO MOUNTAIN, HEALDVILLE TRAIL

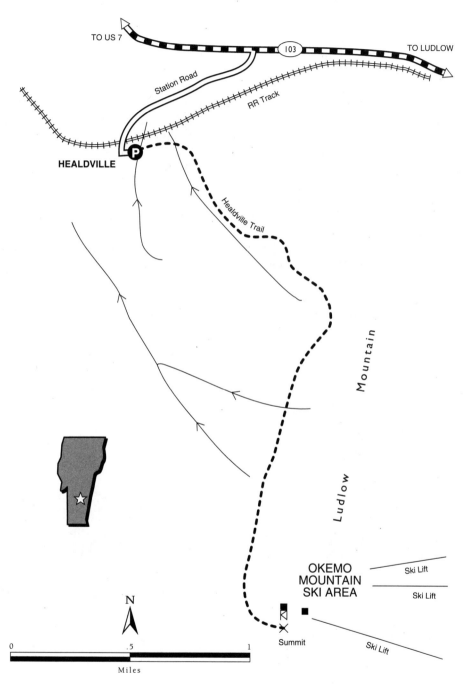

TO US 7

103

TO LUDLOW

Station Road

RR Track

HEALDVILLE

P

Healdville Trail

Mountain

Ludlow

OKEMO
MOUNTAIN
SKI AREA

Ski Lift

Ski Lift

Ski Lift

N

Summit

0   .5   1

Miles

The smooth path rises easily through woods largely devoid of evergreens, but ferns, clubmoss, and wildflowers define the trail below a canopy of hardwood trees. Feeling less like a mountain climb than a walk through a friendly forest, the path briefly swings left (east) about 0.75 mile from the trailhead to abandon the course of the brook and avoid a steeper slope. After veering through switchbacks well marked with double blazes, the path quickly reverts to a western course, rock-hops another brook, and slabs across the slant of the hill to a level mountain shoulder. Well-spaced maples and a damp forest floor make a pleasing wildflower garden on this lightly tilted plateau as the route slides southwest, descends for several yards, and finds a trail sign at the junction of an unnamed path 1 mile from the peak.

Commencing the final leg, the trail drops below a mini-cascade to span the same brook that was abandoned earlier, but promptly rises to resume a moderate march obliquely up the slope. A clearing allows distant views of Killington and the central Green Mountains, as the hike acquires a mountainous feel over the course of the last 0.5 mile. Curling past gnarled birch and bounding up several steep pitches, the narrow path ends at a sign just beyond the chimney of a vanished cabin. Look closely through the trees on the right to spot the fire tower at the summit.

The evergreens that prevent views from this peak also mask ski trails that pass within yards of the top. To enjoy the sights, climb the fire tower stairs and rise above the trees, where a quad chairlift with a UFO look may immediately startle your eye. Howling winds often blow freely through the tower, shivering the boards at your feet and blasting your face from any point of the compass. It's all considered part of the fun. Just brace yourself firmly, grip the rails, and scan concentric circles of mountains for the source of the blustery gales.

General description:	A well-groomed walk from a village park to a bird's-eye view of Woodstock and the Ottauquechee River.
General location:	East-central Vermont, near the middle of Woodstock Village.
Length:	About 3 miles round-trip, with longer options.
Difficulty:	Moderate due to length, but easy grades and excellent footing.
Elevation gain:	500 feet.
Special attractions:	Vermont's best village overlook and surprising glimpses of wildlife.
Maps:	USGS Woodstock, North and Woodstock, South quads.
For more information:	None available.

Finding the trailhead: Depart Interstate 89 at Exit 1 and follow U.S. Highway 4 west 10.5 miles to the center of Woodstock Village. Mountain Avenue intersects the highway 0.1 mile west of the central shopping area directly across the town common from the Windsor County Courthouse and the Woodstock Inn. Turn right on Mountain Ave., pass immediately through a covered bridge, continue straight across River Street, and follow the curve of the road to Faulkner Park, a large lawn with paved walkways 0.3 mile from the common. Park off the street in the areas provided.

The hike: Don't make the mistake of thinking that this long trail up a short hill is just a ho-hum village walk. Superb views, pastoral settings, and a sumptuous aura await on this genteel hike, a natural complement to the architectural perfection of historic Woodstock Village. Located across a covered bridge from the town common, county courthouse, and gracious Woodstock Inn, the Faulkner Trail to the south summit of Mount Tom fosters casual conversation and may surprise lucky hikers with glimpses of wildlife.

The trail departs from both corners at the rear of Faulkner Park. I followed a paved walkway to a finely laid stone wall on the far right (northeast) boundary where a dirt path begins just beyond a pump house in a stand of tall pitch pine. As the crow flies, the distance from the grassy lawn to the top of South Peak can't be more than 0.5 mile, but this easygoing trail features so many switchbacks that the length is more than doubled. Long, looping paths crisscross the face of the hill. Hikers pass benches ideal for resting in the piney shade or listening for the peal of church bells cheerfully announcing midday.

Impatient hikers have worn eroded paths directly up the slope, but steep shortcuts clearly miss the point. This trail demands a leisurely pace. Stroll placidly up the hill, talk to hiking friends, and take the time to appreciate

17 MOUNT TOM, FAULKNER TRAIL

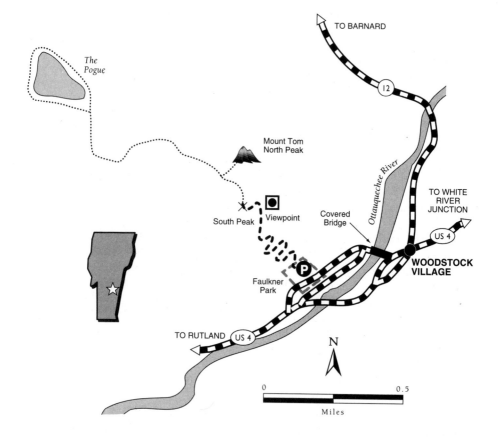

the joys of a sunny day. Glacial erratics pepper the slope, squirrels skitter through trees, and chipmunks peer from carefully crafted stone walls that periodically brace the trail. Soon enough the innumerable switchbacks end at a bench atop a knoll that boasts magnificent views of a storybook New England village.

Anyone wearing street shoes can reach the scenic overlook, but the last push to the top of the hill calls for footwear that's more substantial. Crossing directly over the knoll, the trail dips briefly for 30 yards, then begins the moderate 100-yard climb that ends at the South Peak summit. Stone steps and guywires prevent falls near hazardous drops and make this final segment less difficult than it looks.

The Faulkner Trail ends in the broad swath of a grass-covered carriage road near a log bench with majestic views of Woodstock, the Ottauquechee River, and pastures creeping out of the valleys onto surrounding hills. A host of familiar landmarks fan out below this superior perch—the ellipse of the village green, classic homes of brick, a covered bridge spanning the

A bird's eye-view of Woodstock Village from Mount Tom's southern peak.

twisted river, and the mass of Ludlow Mountain, which draws your attention south.

Explorers with ample time can extend their hike by descending the gradual carriage road northwest from Mount Tom's summit. Passing a spur trail to the top of North Peak (higher, but with restricted views), this elegant path wanders through manicured forests, impressive abutments of stone, and pastoral fields to a small pond called The Pogue. Cattail marshes, mountain views, deer tracks, ducks, and even a cautious red fox seen far across a peaceful meadow can readily make these extra miles the highlight of the hike.

THE GREEN MOUNTAIN NATIONAL FOREST, NORTHERN SECTION

OVERVIEW

Bounded by scenic Vermont Highway 100 and the lowlands of Lake Champlain, the northern half of the Green Mountain National Forest covers 54 miles of rugged ridgeline and two of Vermont's highest peaks. Waterfalls, alpine ponds, skyline trails, an arctic summit, and two wilderness areas crowd this backcountry sector with a superb selection of vigorous climbs and extended overnight hikes.

But this congenial region also embraces an assortment of civilized trails that appeal to less active hikers. The poetry of Robert Frost, a picnic at Texas Falls, falcons nesting on the Great Cliff, and a taste of the backcountry camping good life on the shore of Silver Lake, make the northern section of the Green Mountain National Forest the most pleasure-packed part of the state.

18   ABBEY POND

General description:	A half-day hike to a ridgetop pond; suitable for rainy weather.
General location:	5 miles east of Middlebury.
Length:	3.8 miles round-trip.
Difficulty:	Moderate.
Elevation gain:	1,200 feet.
Special attractions:	Pristine pond, cascading brook, and assorted wildlife.
Maps:	USGS South Mountain quad.
For more information:	Middlebury Ranger District, Route 7, RR 4, Box 1260, Middlebury, VT 05753; (802) 388-4362.

Finding the trailhead: From the junction of Vermont Highways 116 and 125 in East Middlebury, take VT 116 north 2.3 miles to a sign for the Abbey Pond Trail. Turn right onto a gravel road that forks at the edge of the highway and crosses private land. Keep right on the prong that passes a sugar house and ends after 0.3 mile in a stony clearing. Lumber and gravel operations make heavy use of these roads. Don't block the right-of-way. Blue blazes locate the trail, which continues up the road ahead.

The hike: Rain, drizzle, fog—what's a hiker supposed to do? If you're bound and determined to tramp through the woods in spite of inclement weather, an outing to Abbey Pond might be just what you have in mind. As a matter of fact, a gentle shower should even improve this hike. Plumes of mist subtly enhance the mystery of this alpine pond, and liquid sunshine adds some punch to the froth of small cascades.

Rain or shine, the trailhead is disappointing. Walking east up a treeless slope on a rocky extension of the access road, don't be dismayed by the dismal surroundings and the din of a gravel pit. Change comes dramatically as the path squeezes into the forest and serenity again prevails. After only 0.2 mile, a wooden bridge spans the first junction with the outlet brook, where an off-trail scramble 20 yards uphill overlooks a stepping-stone series of bright cascades. Forced sharply right by a stack of giant boulders, the main trail soon teases the northern bank of the brook, which entertains hikers with foamy drops as they work their way upstream.

18 ABBEY POND

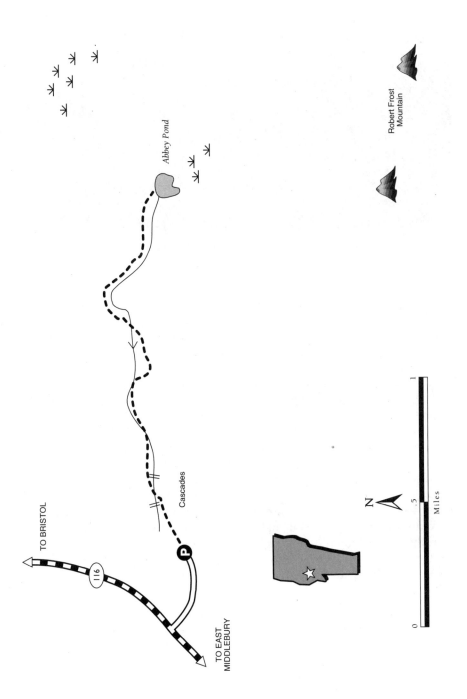

Robert Frost Mountain

Abbey Pond

Cascades

TO BRISTOL

116

TO EAST MIDDLEBURY

N

0 .5 1

Miles

Wetlands and misty mountains, rainy day enchantment at Abbey Pond.

A missing bridge won't faze trampers at the second crossing of the brook where boulders are large and steps come easy. High above the opposite bank, the trail bends left to pursue the stream then climbs steadily through a rock-slide clearing with a fleeting glimpse of the sky. Spinning right and drifting away from the water, the path swings back to the left at its halfway point, avoiding a brush-covered fork that branches to the right.

The bulk of the climbing ends under tall timber near the height of the watershed. The path rejoins the brook just west of the third and final crossing. Tracing a lingering stream through ferns and well-spaced trees, the last 0.6 mile evades several unseen marshes as the trail wanders through muddy terrain to the outlet of Abbey Pond.

Nestled at the base of low mountains, trampled paths make webs in wetland grass, skirt a tadpole inlet, and pass a beaver dam on their way to waterfront viewpoints overlooking this pristine pond. Nature's enchantments unfold on many levels—you may see moose tracks on the trail, lily pads near the dam, silhouettes of a raptor's nest in the branches of a tree, and the misty visage of Robert Frost Mountain keeping close watch over all. Poking about these many mysteries, you may not even notice a little rain.

General description:	A backpack loop to a Green Mountain ridge near the headwaters of the New Haven River.
General location:	About 8 miles east of Middlebury.
Length:	12.8 miles.
Difficulty:	Intermediate.
Elevation gain:	2,200 feet from lowest to highest point, with substantially more gain and loss encountered along the ridge.
Special attractions:	Mountain views, convenient shelters, and secluded wilderness streams.
Maps:	USGS Lincoln quad.
For more information:	Middlebury Ranger District, Route 7, RR 4, Box 1260, Middlebury, VT 05753; (802) 388-4362.

Finding the trailhead: Forest Road 59 runs north from Vermont Highway 125, 0.3 mile west of the Breadloaf Campus of Middlebury College and less than 3 miles east of Ripton. Follow this gravel road 3.6 miles to Steam Mill Clearing, where there is a small parking lot for another trail (see Hike 24). Continue north 1 mile, turn right onto Forest Road 54, then turn right again after 4 miles onto Forest Road 201. The traveled portion of this gravel road ends in 0.4 mile near a primitive campsite and a turnaround loop at the trailhead.

The hike: The Cooley Glen and Emily Proctor trails radiate from a common campsite at the end of a forest road and intersect the Long Trail (LT) at points 5.6 miles apart on the heights of the Green Mountain ridge. A perfect weekend expedition, this triangular circuit enters the Breadloaf Wilderness, circles the headwaters of the New Haven River, passes shelters in mountain cols, and returns to the trailhead through remote woodlands packed with wildlife and mountain streams. With a route past four summits, two valleys, and three tremendous campsites, what more could a hiker ask?

Bearing right from the end of the forest road 3.7 miles from its eastern end at the LT junction, the Emily Proctor Trail wanders into the woods as a slender footpath that climbs out of a hollow, with the symmetrical summit of Mount Cleveland visible on a distant ridge. Quickly finding the overgrown remnants of a former logging road, the path arcs southeast on a brisk ascent that ends at a timbered clearing where a solitary hawk may soar high above the slopes of Bread Loaf Mountain. After striding easily down a broad swath for nearly 0.1 mile, the route turns left at a sign, onto a slimmer path, and maintains a gradual climb.

Evergreens are few and far between as the trail enters the Breadloaf Wilderness on a track that seems to hang from the side of the scenic valley, revealing the scope of the hike ahead. Rimming the skyline in a graceful arch, Mount Wilson, Mount Roosevelt, an unnamed peak, and familiar Mount

Cleveland define the limits of this sylvan watershed that follows the profile of the eastern ridge. A pleasant traipse follows as the trail bends more directly south above a branch of the New Haven River, crisscrosses a stream on its way up a mini-valley, and climbs moderately for a solid mile to a lean-to shelter just south of Mount Wilson's peak.

Plopped in a grassy clearing at the head of a tiny cirque, the Emily Proctor Shelter is an ideal place for an overnight stop, especially for hikers who favor dining in the company of mountain views. When it's time to move on, the LT (heading north) leaves the back of the shelter, relaxes for 0.1 mile, and ambles through spruce and fir before vigorously conquering the worst of Mount Wilson's slope. This unsung peak is the literal high point of the hike, but its knobby top is a fooler. You haven't reached the summit until you stand on a congregation of rocks and find an eastern spur that skips off to a view of Bread Loaf Mountain and a sea of southern peaks.

Descending more than 400 feet from the summit of Mount Wilson, the LT bottoms out in a sag before it climbs a bump on Mount Roosevelt's ridge and meets the Clark Brook Trail 0.4 mile from the top. As the path curls east on this modest peak, hikers pass Killington View, a bulbous outcrop with comfortable ribs that hold you as you bask in the sun and eye the southern scene. A fantastic world surrounds hikers who continue north on this intimate ridge, where spruce and hemlock filter horizons on either side. Random variations in elevation on this multi-knobbed crest also provide an endurance workout until the high ground weaves into another sag then zigzags to an anonymous peak identified only by a crude plaque that reads "Little Hans."

The next 1.6 miles are almost graceful, following a long, smooth, rhythmic descent and a comparable 500-foot climb to Mount Cleveland's summit woods. No views detain hikers on this overgrown peak. Instead, the LT bends northwest in a speedy 0.5 mile descent to the Cooley Glen Shelter, a pleasant but less scenic lean-to only yards from the final junction, where the last 3.5-mile leg of the hike begins.

Stony footing drops the Cooley Glen Trail down from the mountain's heights until traces of a logging route gentle the walk beyond the first crossing of a brook. Of all the abundant streams and rivulets on this rapid downhill jaunt, hikers will most recall a wild, sunny glen filled with bright cascades as the trail curves east, tracking a tributary out of a mountain cirque.

Farther down the slope, as you leave the Breadloaf Wilderness, you will come to another notable crossing. The trail skirts the length of a narrow island caught between parallel streams before it spans the New Haven River on a bridge 0.3 mile from the trailhead. The circuit concludes on a short extension of the gravel forest road from which you started.

19 COOLEY GLEN AND EMILY PROCTOR TRAILS

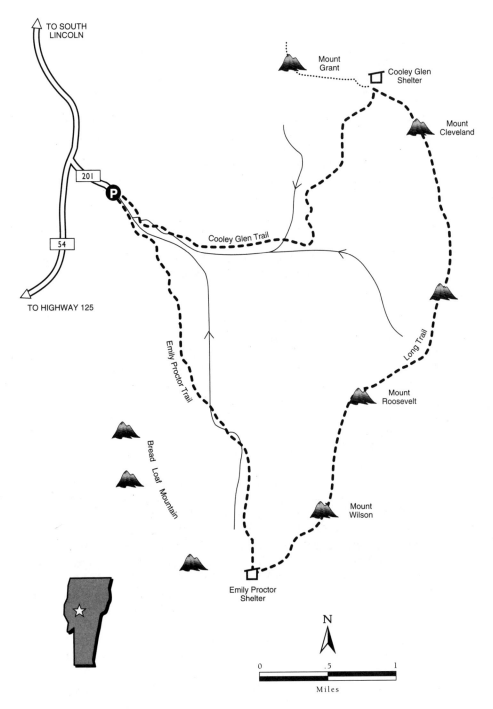

TO SOUTH
LINCOLN

Mount
Grant

Cooley Glen
Shelter

Mount
Cleveland

201

P

Cooley Glen Trail

54

TO HIGHWAY 125

Long Trail

Emily Proctor Trail

Mount
Roosevelt

Bread Loaf Mountain

Mount
Wilson

Emily Proctor
Shelter

N

0   .5   1

Miles

General description:	A short nature walk dedicated to the poetry of Robert Frost. Portions of this trail are barrier free.
General location:	About 13 miles southeast of Middlebury.
Length:	About 1 mile.
Difficulty:	Easy.
Elevation gain:	Negligible.
Special attractions:	Trailside displays with poems that highlight the everyday wonders of New England fields and forests.
Maps:	Handout maps are available from the address below.
For more information:	Middlebury Ranger District, Route 7, RR 4, Box 1260, Middlebury, VT 05753; (802) 388-4362.

Finding the trailhead: The parking area for the Robert Frost Interpretive Trail is on the south side of Vermont Highway 125, 1 mile west of the Breadloaf Campus of Middlebury College and 1.9 miles east of Ripton. Don't be confused by the Robert Frost Wayside Park, 0.3 mile east on the opposite (north) side of the road.

The hike: Just down the road from the Breadloaf Campus of Middlebury College, and less than 1 mile from the cabin where New England's poet lived and worked for twenty-three years, the Robert Frost Trail unquestionably occupies the literary heart of Vermont. Nestled in a high valley that flanks the Middlebury River, this carefully designed, barrier-free trail carries on the Frost tradition through simple signposts that thoughtfully display selections from poems perfectly attuned to their surroundings. This walk isn't just for the bookish crowd; it is a great chance for all to observe the wonders of field and forest through the eyes of a scholarly farmer and accomplished naturalist.

The trail consists of two parts—a barrier-free loop on the north side of the river, and a longer circuit on the far side of a bridge not suitable for the physically impaired. Crushed stones and landscape timbers form much of the barrier-free section that circles right from the parking area and passes over a walkway elevated above a marsh. Poems and benches wait near observation points for relaxed viewing of thickets along the wetlands, native birds in their natural habitat, and comfortable contours of verdant hills that rise to mountains beyond. Turn left at a T to complete the initial loop, or bear right and continue to the banks of the Middlebury River where the barrier-free portion ends at a pleasant overlook at the foot of a wooden bridge.

On the south side of the river, visitors confront an immediate fork in the trail, a conundrum neatly highlighted by the lines of "The Road Not Taken." No need to worry here, though—both prongs of this woodland way loop back to the identical point, but signposts suggest that the path most traveled should lead you to the right.

The southern loop gracefully meanders up an embankment through typical New England woods, edges a large field, and eventually returns to the bridge by tracking beside the river. Along the way signs identify hemlock, spruce, hobblebush, and bracken ferns on an intimate path with enough twists and turns to keep conversations private. Drifting through fields of huckleberries, blueberries, songbirds, and meadowsweet, hikers find a wooden map etched with profiles of surrounding mountains and selections of poetry well suited to a nature hike. I won't give away all the surprises, but "Something For Hope" is a well-placed ode to field/forest succession, and completion of the trail takes on new meaning as it ends, thoughtfully, with "Reluctance."

20 ROBERT FROST INTERPRETIVE TRAIL

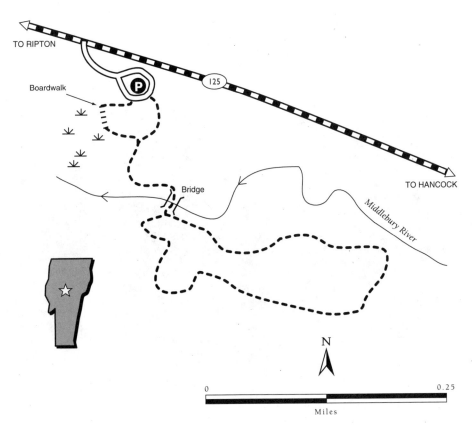

General description:	A short hike to a clifftop ledge overlooking Brandon Gap.
General location:	East of U.S. Highway 7 between Rutland and Middlebury.
Length:	1.2 miles round-trip.
Difficulty:	Moderate.
Elevation gain:	600 feet.
Special attractions:	Peregrine falcons and scenic views.
Maps:	USGS Mount Carmel quad.
For more information:	Rochester Ranger District, Route 100, RR 2, Box 35, Rochester, VT 05767; (802) 767-4261.

Finding the trailhead: Locate the Long Trail parking lot on the south side of Vermont Highway 73, 9.1 miles west of Vermont Highway 100 (near Rochester), or 6.3 miles east of U.S. Highway 7 (near Brandon). The trailhead is across the road.

The hike: A wall of stone rising 700 feet above the highway through Brandon Gap, the Great Cliff of Mount Horrid draws travelers to a roadside outlook like a magnetic force. High above a marshy meadow and the ripples of a beaver pond, the sheer face of this birch-speckled summit rises from crumbling scree, a giant throne for tiny hikers crouched on its soaring ledge.

Gazing into Bradford Gap from the edge of the Great Cliff.

A visit to this perch is easier than it looks, and great family entertainment, but there is a curious catch. In recent years, peregrine falcons have returned to these towering cliffs. From March through the middle of summer, signs at the trailhead provide early warning if portions of trail are closed to protect their nests.

Like many hikes that begin in Green Mountain passes, the hardest part of this climb comes first, as the Long Trail (LT) ducks under power lines, turns left, and completes the short, steep scamper out of Brandon Gap. Corkscrew switchbacks through the heart of a sugarbush soon establish a moderate pace before the trail angles upward on a southwestern contour in a sunny grove of birch. Zigzag loops and a second rapid ascent elevate the path to a ridge covered by bedrock slabs and wind-gnarled trees. A sloping crown briefly rises toward the summit at a docile pitch. Stone steps then

21 MOUNT HORRID AND THE GREAT CLIFF

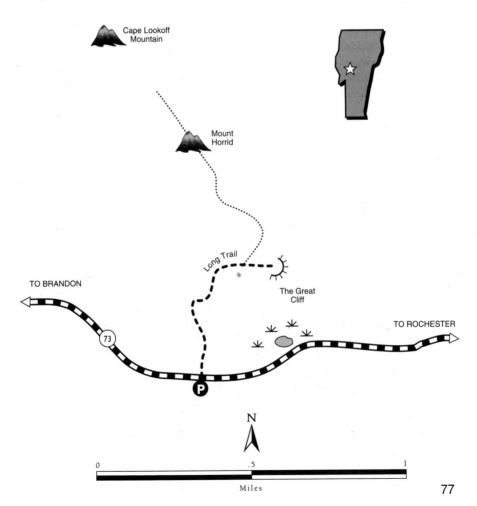

TO BRANDON

TO ROCHESTER

Cape Lookoff
Mountain

Mount
Horrid

Long Trail

The Great
Cliff

73

P

N

0   .5   1

Miles

carry the trail sharply upward past an outcrop on the right until the spur path to the Great Cliff intersects at the top of the rough-hewn stairs.

Bearing right, the blue-blazed spur rises steadily for several yards and then gently drops to a broad ledge lining the top of the Great Cliff. Settle your pack in a seam of rock and explore the wide-angle views that blossom from this towering cornice. To the left, Vermont Highway 73 follows Brandon Brook into hills that meld to the east. To the right, Brandon Gap opens a doorway to the Champlain Valley, while across the way Goshen Mountain forms the southern wall of the pass, keeping watch over toy-sized cars in the turnout by the beaver marsh.

This hike is over so quickly, people often stand at the clifftop feeling all dressed up with no place to go. One simple solution: push on to the top of the mountain! From the head of the stairs, the LT bears left on a calm 0.6-mile walk through mature woods just below the top of the ridge, safe from gusty winds that buffet the open cliffs. The solitary walk passes a spur to an attractive, uncrowded western vista and ends at Mount Horrid's wooded summit with a side path to limited views. The end isn't overly exciting, but the reward lies in healthy exertion and the quiet satisfaction of not leaving a hike half done.

22 MONROE SKYLINE, LINCOLN GAP TO APPALACHIAN GAP

General description:	A one-way backpack along a celebrated section of a scenic Green Mountain ridge.
General location:	About 20 miles southwest of Montpelier.
Length:	11.6 miles one way.
Difficulty:	Intermediate.
Elevation gain:	1,700 feet from lowest to highest point, with substantially more gain and loss encountered along the ridge.
Special attractions:	Stunning views, rare alpine plants, and two of Vermont's five highest peaks.
Maps:	USGS Lincoln and Mount Ellen quads.
For more information:	Middlebury Ranger District, Route 7, RR 4, Box 1260, Middlebury, VT 05753; (802) 388-4362.

Finding the trailhead: This hike links two well-marked Long Trail (LT) parking lots. At the southern end in Lincoln Gap, the LT intersects the seasonal Lincoln-Warren Highway 4.8 miles east of Lincoln or 4.5 miles west of Vermont Highway 100 in Warren. At the northern end in Appalachian Gap, the LT crosses Vermont Highway 17, 9.5 miles east of Vermont Highway 116 or 6.4 miles west of VT 100 just south of Waitsfield.

22 MONROE SKYLINE, LINCOLN GAP TO APPALACHIAN GAP

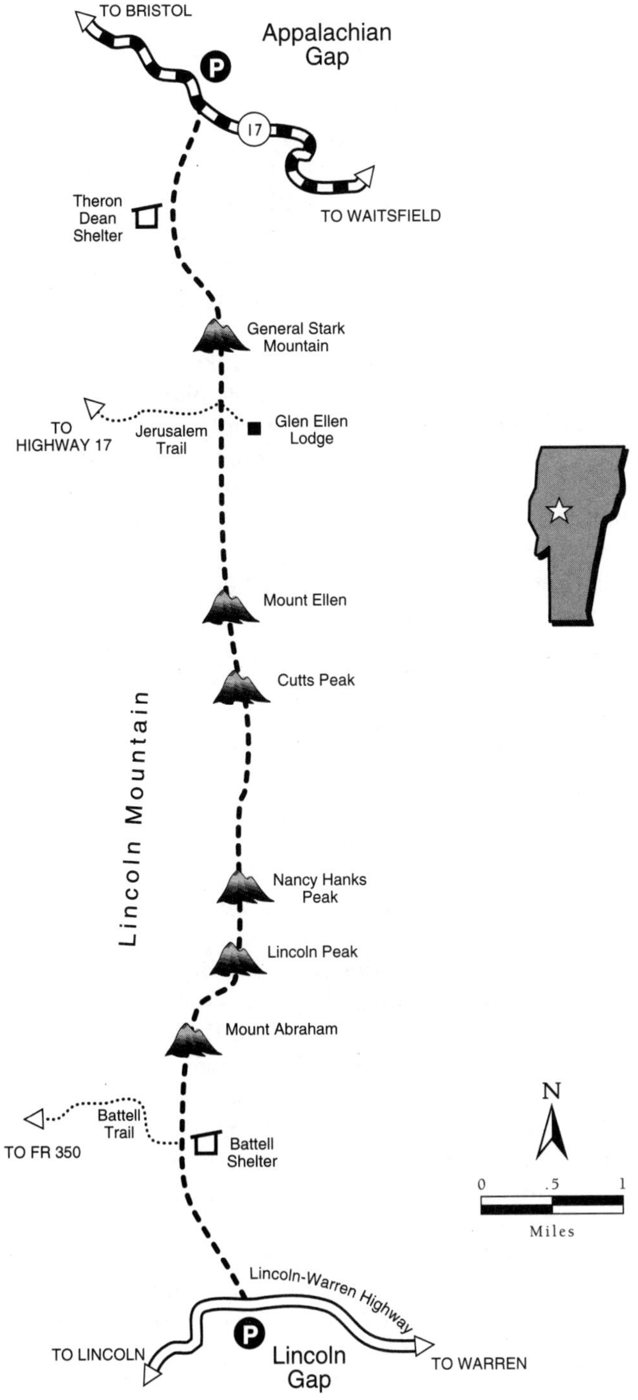

TO BRISTOL

Appalachian Gap

P

17

TO WAITSFIELD

Theron Dean Shelter

General Stark Mountain

TO HIGHWAY 17

Jerusalem Trail

Glen Ellen Lodge

Mount Ellen

Cutts Peak

Lincoln Mountain

Nancy Hanks Peak

Lincoln Peak

Mount Abraham

Battell Trail

TO FR 350

Battell Shelter

N

0   .5   1

Miles

Lincoln-Warren Highway

P

TO LINCOLN

Lincoln Gap

TO WARREN

The hike: Although the Long Trail (LT) stretches 265 miles from Massachusetts to the Canadian border, its 30-mile segment from Lincoln Gap to the Winooski River, known as the Monroe Skyline, captures a generous portion of Vermont's finest alpine sights. This overnight trek along a narrow section of the Green Mountain ridge from Lincoln Gap to Appalachian Gap features a shortened version of the Skyline route, a popular traverse widely regarded as a highlight of the famous hike.

Cooperation is needed to spot a car at the end of this paradoxical journey that rambles over six summits yet visits only two mountains, Lincoln (with five peaks) and General Stark. Spanning arctic heights adorned with alpine plants, this northbound traverse clearly reminds hikers of the need for conservation. It also proves that natural environs can be scenic though not pristine. Three major ski areas (Sugarbush North, Sugarbush South, and Mad River Glen) pepper the eastern slopes that parallel much of this hike, providing clearings that are necessary for marvelous views. Other improvements are specifically intended to benefit LT hikers. Convenient shelters near both ends of this elevated tour allow flexible planning for late starters, early starters, and one or more nights on the trail.

Fresh legs are a plus at Lincoln Gap. Beginning at an elevation of 2,424 feet, the trail scrambles up and over a knoll before beginning the steep and rocky ascent that leads to the Battell Shelter and the 4,006-foot summit of Mount Abraham after 2.6 miles. Rare plants and spectacular views grace this special peak, which can also be approached on the Battell Trail (see Hike 24).

Though hardly a walk in the park, the rest of the northward march gives hikers a comparative break as the path rolls along the mountain's slender crest gaining and losing elevation in only modest chunks. Dipping less than 200 feet, the LT encounters the first vestige of ski terrain when it bounces over a subordinate summit known as Little Abe and rises to Lincoln Peak, finding vistas that encircle the former site of a skiers' gondola lift. Veering left into the woods beyond the view, the route casually descends 0.6 mile to the smaller Nancy Hanks Peak, undulates north, and curls behind a chairlift before steadily ascending to an outlook on Cutts Peak at the approximate midpoint of the hike.

In the next 0.4 mile, friendly grades carry the LT to its highest elevation on this hike as the ridge first sags then climbs less than 100 feet to attain the summit of Glen Ellen, the third highest peak in the state. (See Hike 42 for detailed descriptions of the exceptional views from this open top and the path that descends nearly 600 feet to the Jerusalem Trail.) For overnight camping with stupendous sunrise views, trek an additional 0.1 mile north from the Jerusalem Trail junction and bear right on the Barton Trail, a short spur that drops 0.2 mile to a simple log shelter known as the Glen Ellen Lodge.

Stark Mountain poses the final obstacle on your journey, a narrow, mile-long band that incorporates ski runs into the route. The trail first pops to its highest top with a short, steep climb of General Stark. It then cruises an arched crest to vistas from a chairlift station open to campers in summer months. Ski swaths meld as the LT nudges the end of the northern ridge before rapidly falling over a ledge to the Theron Dean Shelter, a bunk space near a spur to its own panorama and underground "cave." Departing these final attractions, the trek concludes by passing another chairlift, skimming another ski trail garnished ridge, and dropping 900 feet in 1.8 miles to vehicles waiting at Appalachian Gap.

23 *RATTLESNAKE CLIFFS, THE FALLS OF LANA, AND SILVER LAKE*

General description:	A collection of trails to mountain views and waterfront camps for day hikers and backpackers alike.
General location:	8 miles southeast of Middlebury.
Length:	Variable, 1 to 4.7 miles round-trip.
Difficulty:	Easy to moderate.
Elevation gain:	1,100 feet to Rattlesnake Cliff.
Special attractions:	The Falls of Lana, clifftop views, and campsites on a mountain lake.
Maps:	USGS East Middlebury quad.
For more information:	Middlebury Ranger District, Route 7, RR 4, Box 1260, Middlebury, VT 05753; (802) 388-4362.

Finding the trailhead: Forest Dale lies at the junction of Vermont Highways 53 and 73, 14 miles west of Vermont Highway 100 and 3 miles east of U.S. Highway 7. Follow VT 53 north 5.2 miles from Forest Dale to a new, large parking turnout for Silver Lake and the Falls of Lana on the right.

The hike: A national magazine recently touted Silver Lake as one of the fifteen best springtime campsites in the country. Its standards were right on track, but its season was too confined. In fact, the lakes, campgrounds, trails, and mountains that pack this scenic region make Mount Moosalamoo and Silver Lake great vacation playgrounds any time of year. Outdoor options in the area are overwhelming, and the paths described here are suited to all hikers, whether taking a break from Branbury Beach or those trekking through the forest to an overnight lakeside camp.

First stop on this varied hike: the foamy Falls of Lana. Scramble 50 yards up a path from the parking loop, turn right onto a gravel track, and quickly find a welcoming sign to the Silver Lake Recreation Area. An easily walked trail swings sharply left beyond the sign as it weaves upward through a forest coated with a patchwork of stones and boulders. A brief view of Lake Dunmore flashes by on the left as the trail slides under a power line and finds the Falls of Lana waiting on the opposite side. Use caution as you

The Rattlesnake Cliffs, overlooking Lake Dunmore and the far Adirondacks.

23 RATTLESNAKE CLIFFS, THE FALLS OF LANA, AND SILVER LAKE

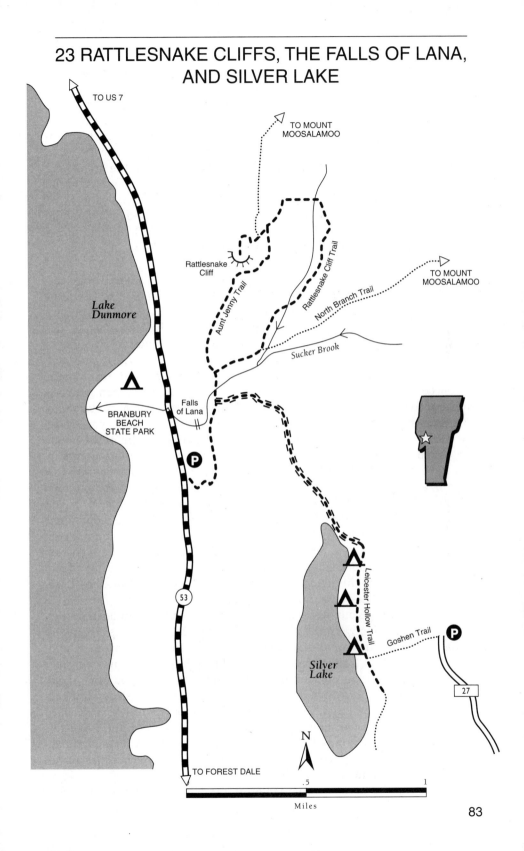

TO US 7

TO MOUNT MOOSALAMOO

Rattlesnake Cliff

Lake Dunmore

Aunt Jenny Trail

Rattlesnake Cliff Trail

North Branch Trail

TO MOUNT MOOSALAMOO

Sucker Brook

BRANBURY BEACH STATE PARK

Falls of Lana

P

53

Leicester Hollow Trail

Goshen Trail

P

27

Silver Lake

N

TO FOREST DALE

.5   1

Miles

approach the dangerous dropoffs into the bowels of Sucker Brook, which gushes through a blocky cleft and combines with Lake Dunmore, and the Adirondacks in a single stunning scene.

Continuing north from the falls, the path chases cascades and tiny pools until it meets a major intersection complete with trail signs and a comfort station. (I'll call this "Privy Junction.") The road to Silver Lake curls southeast from here but, for now, the views from Rattlesnake Cliffs are the focus of our attention. Track upstream another 75 yards and cross the brook on a wooden bridge following signs for Rattlesnake Point. On the far side of the stream, turn right at a sign for the Falls of Lana Picnic Area and walk 25 yards to a second junction. To the left, trails descend to the northwest side of the falls, Branbury State Park, and Vermont Highway 53. To the right, a network of trails circles 1.8 miles to Rattlesnake Cliff, Mount Moosalamoo, and beyond.

The route courses northeast on an old logging grade slightly removed from the west bank of the stream, passes the lower junction of the Aunt Jenny Trail, and avoids the North Branch Trail, which forks right in a brushy clearing. Now 1.5 miles from its destination, the first half of the broad Rattlesnake Cliff Trail roughly follows the deep ravine of a tributary that remains largely hidden except at crossings near the bottom of the ridge and later close to the top. After the second crossing, the path loops west, turns south on easy contours, meets the upper end of the Aunt Jenny Trail, then switches back past rocky outcrops to a junction with the Moosalamoo Mountain trail 0.3 mile from the cliffs. Burgeoning views grab your attention as you zigzag down to the level of the open ledge and placidly stroll the rim of the precipice. Amid forests speckled with fields of corn, Lake Dunmore points to Fern Lake and the length of the Vermont Valley to the south, while the Taconics and Adirondacks form a barrier to the west. The most astounding sight is the image of Silver Lake floating magically above the valley, caught in the folds of a wooded ridge just west of Worth and Romance mountains.

A worn path leads beyond the lookout to a very precarious scramble on an upper level of cliffs. Better to backtrack to the top of the zigzag pitch and bear left on a safer spur that ends at the highest point. Don't miss this added excursion that spotlights tremendous views of the rounded head of Lake Dunmore and impressive Adirondack peaks.

To save retracing your steps all the way to the picnic grounds, try a descent on the Aunt Jenny Trail, a slightly rougher path that returns directly to the Rattlesnake Cliff Trail north of the bridge above the falls. Anyone who'd like to explore Silver Lake should return to Privy Junction. Signs point the way along a gravel road that climbs a steady mile up the impounding ridge to a dam, picnic area, and campground clustered at the north end of the lake. From the campground, walk 0.1 mile along a four-wheel-drive road as it weaves under a power line and then turn right (south) on the Leicester Hollow Trail that runs parallel to the eastern shore. Take your pick of secluded Silver Lake sites where towering pines and gravel beaches make family camping an uncompromising treat.

If walk-in tenting is your primary interest, the campground can be reached through a back door. From VT 53, drive 1.7 miles east on VT 73, turn north on Forest Road 32, then go west on Forest Road 27. From the east parking area, Silver Lake campsites are 0.6 mile west on the Goshen Trail.

24 SKYLIGHT POND TRAIL, BATTELL AND BREAD LOAF MOUNTAINS

General description:	A day hike to summits in the Breadloaf Wilderness with an overnight option in a cabin on an alpine lake.
General location:	About 10 miles east of Middlebury.
Length:	6.8 miles round-trip.
Difficulty:	Intermediate.
Elevation gain:	1,900 feet.
Special attractions:	Skylight Pond, Skyline Lodge, and western mountain views.
Maps:	USGS Bread Loaf and Lincoln quads.
For more information:	Middlebury Ranger District, Route 7, RR 4, Box 1260, Middlebury, VT 05753; (802) 388-4362.

Finding the trailhead: Forest Road 59 runs north from Vermont Highway 125, 0.3 mile west of the Breadloaf Campus of Middlebury College and less than 3 miles east of Ripton. Follow this gravel road 3.6 miles to trailhead parking at Steam Mill Clearing.

The hike: Boasting few superlatives, the path to Skylight Pond still ranks among the most popular trails in the state. Wooded peaks, middling mountains, and pleasant but restricted views don't usually add up to a favored destination, but a choice of summits, an alpine pond, and one of the Long Trail's (LT) newest lodges transform this temperate trail into a champion of midrange hikes.

The straightforward 2.3-mile climb from Steam Mill Clearing to the LT junction near Skylight Pond begins on a docile track that passes a registration box after 100 yards then doubles that distance to meet a bend in a woodland stream. Soon swinging right to cross the flow, the trail bears southeast, spans a larger brook on a hiker's bridge 0.2 mile from the trailhead, and remains almost level until it jumps the first of several seasonal streams. A moderate ascent soon carries hikers into the Breadloaf Wilderness, a 21,000-acre preserve that envelops the LT from VT 125 nearly to Lincoln Gap. Changing course only to avoid gullies and maintain a steady gait, the trail wiggles east with an escalating number of twists and turns that correspond to the gradual increase in pitch. Climbing muscles feel well used by the time the path rolls onto the top of the rounded ridge and crosses the LT in a shallow col between Battell and Bread Loaf mountains.

Choices abound at this LT junction. For instant gratification, turn right (south) and troop less than 200 yards uphill to the summit of Battell Mountain. Here, an unmarked spur wends 70 yards back down to a craggy outcrop with a very good western view. Check out the Champlain Valley, Taconic Range, and distant peaks in New York, but don't ignore Bread Loaf Mountain, that nearby rounded summit blocking the northern view.

If Bread Loaf strikes your fancy, prepare for a vigorous effort. Return to the shallow col and travel the LT north as it rolls over an easy knoll and descends in staggered stages to the base of the mountain's crown. In the steepest 0.2-mile scramble of the day, the rocky path bounces up a south-facing slope and gains the flat top of the summit, where hiking greatly improves. After strolling 0.7 mile across the conifer-coated peak, the trail adds a hairpin turn. A scenic detour leaves the apex of the curve bearing toward another lookout crag. Far below, the headwaters of the Middlebury River convene in unspoiled wilderness east of the Champlain Valley, while Worth Mountain and Middlebury Gap make a spectacle to the south.

For leisurely exploration of this region, an overnight stay at Skyline Lodge

24 SKYLIGHT POND TRAIL, BATTELL AND BREAD LOAF MOUNTAINS

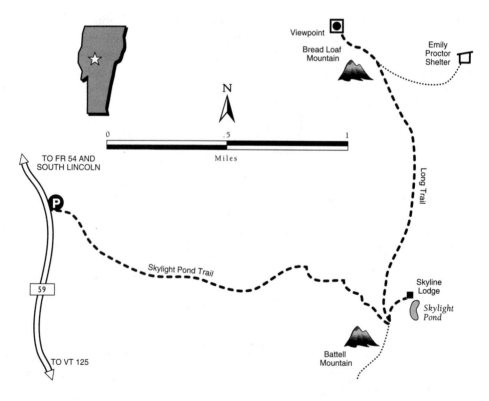

Skyline Lodge, Long Trail comfort between Battell and Bread Loaf mountains.

really can't be beat. An extension of the Skylight Pond Trail runs east 0.1 mile from the last LT junction to this double-decker, peeled log cabin just below the crest of the ridge overlooking a mountain lake. Twanging frogs and a full horizon of eastern mountains let you know you're getting close to this perfect spot to welcome the dawn of another day.

25   TEXAS FALLS RECREATION AREA

General description:	A short exploration of a small river gorge and nearby nature trail. Barrier-free access to fishing is also provided.
General location:	Southeast of Middlebury and northeast of Rutland, in the heart of Green Mountain National Forest.
Length:	1 mile.
Difficulty:	Easy.
Elevation gain:	200 feet.
Special attractions:	Cascades and pools on the Hancock Branch of the White River.
Maps:	USGS Bread Loaf quad, or handout maps available from the address below.
For more information:	Rochester Ranger District, Route 100, RR 2, Box 35, Rochester, VT 05767; (802) 767-4261.

Finding the trailhead: From the junction of Vermont Highways 100 and 125 in Hancock, drive 3 miles west on VT 125 and turn right onto Forest Road 39. Parking for Texas Falls is on the left 0.5 mile north up FR 39. Picnic grounds and walk-in campsites are located beyond the falls.

The hike: Cascades tumbling through a rocky gorge lure visitors to the Texas Falls Recreation Area. Primitive campsites, barrier-free fishing, attractive picnic grounds, and a pleasant nature trail conspire to keep them there. Located on the principal highway that crosses the northern lobe of Green Mountain National Forest, this convenient haven on the Hancock Branch of the White River strongly appeals to travelers anxious for a wayside rest.

Stroll a few paces down a gravel path from the edge of the access road and the stone posts of a wooden fence line to an observation point above the scenic falls. Cool breezes waft up from the darkness of a deep cleft as stairs on the right descend to a hiker's bridge spanning a narrow chasm. During the summer, a surprisingly delicate stream plunges through a series of small cascades, swirling over polished rock undercut by eddies that have spun since glacial time. From the emerald green depths of an upper pool, the flow slithers and splashes to a hole almost directly under your feet until the current escapes beneath the bridge in a final constricted rush.

On the far side of the gorge, the path bounces up the opposite bank to a bench overlooking the upper pool and readily finds the nature trail loop that departs either left or right. If you don't want to hike the entire loop, turn right and descend to a spur that ends at a second observation point downstream of the falls. Too many visitors miss this fine perspective on the roiling cascades that swoop below the bridge at the climax of Texas Falls.

To hike the complete nature trail loop, turn left above the falls on a path that edges the stony stream for about 200 yards, before it rises 60 feet above the flow and descends to meet Forest Road 39, 0.25 mile up the road. From this junction across from the picnic grounds, the nature trail swings right on a well-groomed path that circles to the top of a hill clad in hemlock, maple, and birch together with varied denizens of the forest's understory. Wide planks guide the trail across wetlands that dot the upper slopes before the path spans several log bridges and two oversized sets of stairs on its return to river level. Be sure to check out the spur path to the downstream observation point before retracing your steps across the bridge above the shaded falls

25 TEXAS FALLS RECREATION AREA

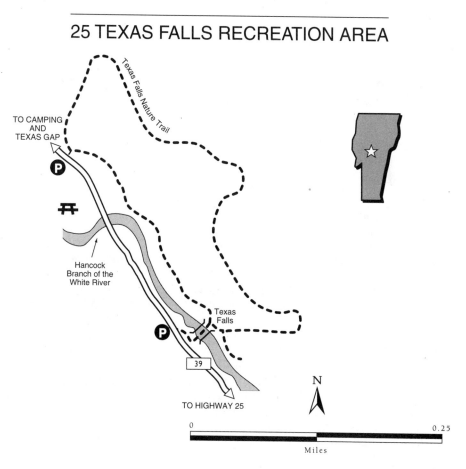

TO CAMPING
AND
TEXAS GAP

Texas Falls Nature Trail

Hancock
Branch of the
White River

Texas
Falls

39

TO HIGHWAY 25

N

0   0.25

Miles

THE CHAMPLAIN LOWLANDS

OVERVIEW

From the Missisquoi Delta to South Bay, two-thirds of the western border of Vermont traces the coast of Lake Champlain. The Champlain Lowlands fill a wide basin that once formed the floor of Lake Vermont and the bottom of an arctic sea. A visible record of the Earth's history permeates this bountiful region. Whether wetland deltas on the Canadian border, endangered species on Shaw Mountain, gravel beaches on Mount Philo, or a coral reef on Button Bay, the secrets of the Champlain Lowlands provide insights into plate tectonics, glaciation, and changes in the natural world.

The lowlands also chronicle human history. Long a corridor for convenient travel, Lake Champlain occupied center stage during the founding of Vermont and the struggle for American independence. At the intervale homestead of Ethan Allen or the coastal heights of Mount Independence, quiet walks in these storied landscapes recall events of history that shaped our present era.

26   ETHAN ALLEN HOMESTEAD, PENINSULA TRAIL

General description:	A short walk through the woods and fields of a historic Vermont homestead.
General location:	About 4 miles north of downtown Burlington.
Length:	1.75 miles.
Difficulty:	Easy.
Elevation gain:	Negligible.
Special attractions:	Historic home, orientation center, and a river intervale.
Maps:	Handout maps are available from the address below; also USGS Colchester quad.
For more information:	Winooski Valley Park District, Ethan Allen Homestead, Burlington, Vermont, 05401; (802) 863-5744.

Finding the trailhead: From U.S. Highway 7 in downtown Burlington, turn west onto Pearl Street and then north onto Vermont Highway 127 (North Champlain Street). Stay on VT 127 as it twists and turns through lights and intersections, following signs for the Ethan Allen Homestead. Take the North Avenue, Beaches exit and turn right onto an access road just before the exit ramp crosses over the highway. Parking is available at the Hill-Brownell Education Center, or hikers can continue through the parking lot, turn left

26 ETHAN ALLEN HOMESTEAD, PENINSULA TRAIL

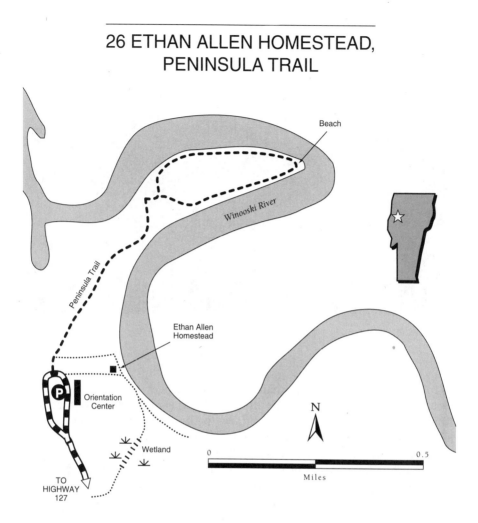

onto the driveway, and park at the bottom of the hill near a metal gate marked with bike path signs.

The hike: If George Washington is the father of our country, then Ethan Allen must surely be regarded the father of Vermont. An audacious mix of land speculator and militia leader, Allen quickly embroiled himself in the conflict with New York over competing claims to real estate throughout the New Hampshire Grants (later Vermont). One thing lead to another, of course—he soon found himself with a price on his head, leading the unauthorized capture of Fort Ticonderoga, and in British imprisonment after certain misadventures in Montreal. When the Revolution ended, Allen returned to an independent Republic of Vermont and settled this Burlington homestead only two years before his death.

Ethan Allen's intervale on the banks of the Winooski River.

In spite of his escapades, Ethan Allen clearly never lost his eye for a fine piece of land. Sited above the tightly coiled bends of the muddy Winooski River, his post-and-beam home stands on the lip of a low promontory overlooking what Allen proudly described as rich upland meadow and choice intervale. Accessed by a web of trails that pass near the modest farmstead, the broad sweep of this fruitful valley remains equally impressive today.

Beginning at a gate near a bike path sign, the Peninsula Trail explores the most pastoral portion of the homestead scene. It angles across a fertile, river bottom plain on a track that points to a cluster of forest ahead. There's sunshine, wind, and room to run on this spacious swath of land until the lane converges with the river as it nears the wooded point. Caught in a sharp bend, the trail rims the peninsula's banks, passes a beach in the crux of the curve (when water levels are low), and reconnects near the neck of the point, forming a natural loop.

If this easy trail doesn't satisfy your outdoor urges, an elevated wetland walk explores a marsh on the opposite side of the house, where the homestead and river loops also provide more extended hiking options. For many people, though, carefree hiking is really an afterthought. Archaeological exhibits, historic orientation, and a multimedia show draw visitors to a modern education center that complements guided tours of a fully reconstructed 1787 home. Trails are free and accessible year-round, but admission is charged for the historic attractions, open mid-May to mid-October.

Ethan Allen Homestead Park is owned by the Winooski Valley Park District, which maintains a string of recreational facilities in several towns within the Winooski River watershed. Birders, bikers, and cross-country skiers should contact the district at the address above for further information about other parks in the area.

27 BUTTON BAY STATE PARK

General description:	A short walk to a coral reef on a point in Lake Champlain. Portions of the hike are barrier free.
General location:	Near Vergennes, about 20 miles south of Burlington.
Length:	1.4 miles round-trip.
Difficulty:	Easy.
Elevation gain:	Nominal.
Special attractions:	Waterfowl, fossils, nature center, and shore views.
Maps:	Handout maps are available at the park or from the address below.
For more information:	Agency of Natural Resources, Department of Forests, Parks and Recreation, District II, RR 2, Box 2161, Pittsford, VT 05763-9713; (802) 483-2314.

Finding the trailhead: From the traffic lights in the center of Vergennes, drive south on Vermont Highway 22A, turn right at the second set of blinking lights onto Panton Road, and turn right once again 2 miles later onto Basin Harbor Road. Follow signs for Button Bay State Park at a left turn after an additional 4.5 miles. The park entrance will appear on the right within 0.8 mile.

The trailhead is located at the end of the park road. Stop at the contact station and proceed past two campgrounds to a gravel parking lot on the left, opposite a pool and picnic area.

The hike: Equatorial shelf, glacial bed, and floor of an arctic sea, Button Bay has done it all. The hiking area in this book least typical of Vermont, this once-tropical reef on the shore of Lake Champlain contains some of the world's oldest fossilized coral and serves as a popular haven for assorted waterfowl. While hikers examine sea snails in limestone near the coast, watch birds flock to the bay, or bask in the stunning views, they also discover the results of plate tectonics and how sediments fashioned the "button molds" that gave this bay its name.

A barrier-free campground, picnic area, and pool distract many happy visitors from the natural core of this park, an easy exploration of the shallow edge of the bay and the magnificent cedar-clad point that juts toward Button Island. From a stop sign near the end of the parking lot, walk along a gravel drive (reserved for handicap vehicles) that skims across a shorefront lawn on the fringe of the picnic grounds. Amid shimmering panoramas of Lake Champlain and blue mountains in the haze, take a few minutes to

27 BUTTON BAY STATE PARK

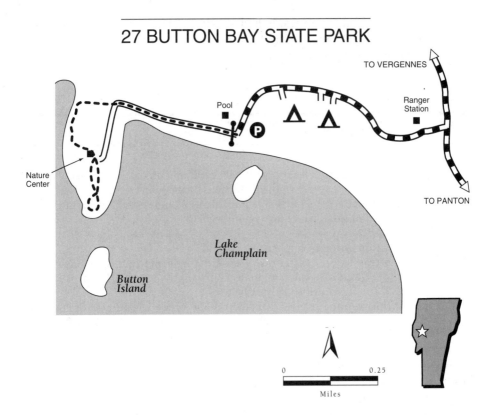

detour down wooden steps on the left and stroll through pungent mudflats teeming with saw grass, cattails, ducks, and timid herons.

Back on the gravel track, upland grasses and small oaks line the breezy arch of the bay while hikers enjoy southern views of waterfowl shielded in an island's lee. As the road turns left toward the nature center, a handy bench allows relaxed birding down the length of the sweeping shore, and the Champlain Trail ventures right to begin an enticing loop. Scooting under huge hemlocks, the trail wanders to the opposite side of the point where fossilized shells and glacial striations adorn white slashes of limestone rock. Remember, though, as you search for these bits of history, collecting natural artifacts is strictly against the rules. Boulders, moss, and cedar abound where the trail touches the coast of this glorious lake that stretches beyond the scope of your vision to mountain landscapes in the north.

The Champlain Trail ends at the stone Nature Museum, where a grassy path off the front porch provides access to the point. Within 100 yards the trail carves a figure eight as it crosses a barrier-free path and ends on water-worn bedrock lapped by the surging lake. I could spend hours in such a spot. Squadrons of geese careen and squabble as their flights come in and out, water broils to a froth in windy chop, the shore divides behind your back, and endless rows of whitecaps underscore the majestic grandeur of Adirondack and Green Mountain peaks.

The Champlain coast at Button Bay.

28   GREEN MOUNTAIN AUDUBON NATURE CENTER, SENSORY TRAIL

General description:	A special path for the visually impaired; also nature trails for the entire family.
General location:	Between Burlington and Montpelier, a few miles west of Camel's Hump.
Length:	0.25 mile.
Difficulty:	Easy.
Elevation gain:	Less than 100 feet.
Special attractions:	Wildlife, diverse habitats, and a sugar house in season.
Maps:	Handout maps are available at the visitor center or from the address below.
For more information:	Green Mountain Audubon Nature Center, 255 Huntington Road, Huntington, VT 05462; (802) 434-3068.

Finding the trailhead: From Exit 11 off Interstate 89, drive 1.7 miles east on U.S. Highway 2 to a traffic light in the center of Richmond. Turn right (south) onto Bridge Street and cross the railroad tracks. Measured from the traffic lights in the center of town, bear right after 0.6 mile, straight after 1.3 miles, left after 1.5 miles, and left after 3.6 miles, all the while staying on the main road and following signs toward Huntington. Turn right onto Sherman Hollow Road after 5.1 miles. Visitor center parking is just 0.2 mile farther on the left.

The hike: Nestled in crinkled foothills near a bend in the Huntington River, more than 5 miles of Green Mountain Audubon Nature Center trails probe a delectable cross-section of classic Vermont terrain. Old meadows, riverbanks, beaver ponds and a hemlock marsh lie below wooded hillsides and active sugar bush, preserving a marvelous mix of habitats for curious younger children or inquisitive naturalists. In a wide array of optional hikes, I especially enjoyed the boardwalk through the heart of the hemlock marsh and a short junket on the fern trail, greatly aided by a superior identification guide.

Workshops, educational programs, and summer ecology camps draw plenty of folks to the nature center, where casual visitors find trail maps and information in a rustic shed. Trails are open from dawn to dusk throughout the year. It's even fun to visit in March, when a lively sugar house springs into Sunday operation.

Designed for the visually impaired, the easily walked Sensory Trail brims with small discoveries whether visitors are sighted or not. Echoing with constant reminders of the wonders of the natural world, this trail pleases any hiker receptive to the sounds, aromas, and textures of everyday Vermont. Beginning from the steps of the nature center deck, a guide rope

28 GREEN MOUNTAIN AUDUBON NATURE CENTER, SENSORY TRAIL

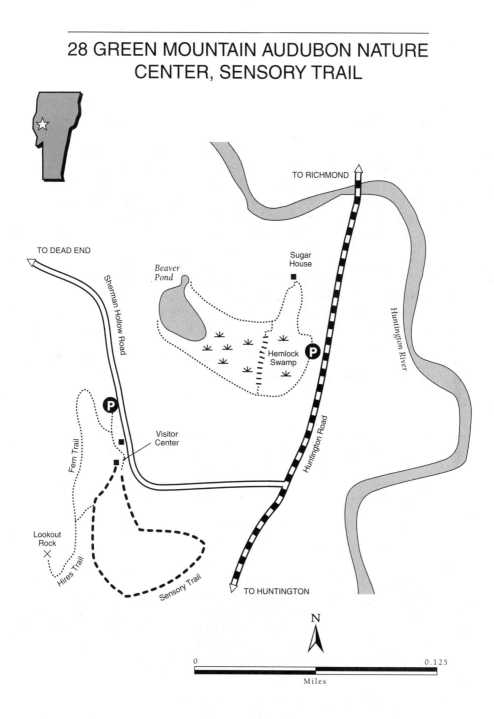

TO RICHMOND

TO DEAD END

Sugar
House

*Beaver
Pond*

Sherman Hollow Road

Hemlock
Swamp

Huntington River

Fern Trail

Visitor
Center

Huntington Road

Lookout
Rock

Hires Trail

Sensory Trail

TO HUNTINGTON

N

0   0.125

Miles

strung through cedar posts lines a path that leads past raised beds of pungent herbs and follows a swath of grass separating woodlands from an overgrown field. Close your eyes with a hand on the escort rope and walk along a trail that parts the middle of a sidehill pasture. Chirping birds and noisy crickets assault your listening ears while the fiery sun warms your face and strengthens the tangy smell of ferns and evergreens that define approaching woods.

Cool air on your skin and soft duff beneath your feet mark a 90-degree turn as the trail enters the forest and launches a sprightly climb to a breezy ridge. Well-spaced benches allow rest in strategic locations as the path performs a looping return in the depths of growing woods. Sighted hikers will appreciate a simple 0.1 mile diversion at the junction with the Hires Trail. Turn left and march uphill to Lookout Rock where another bench permits contemplation of Camel's Hump, a backdrop to local peaks. The Sensory Trail continues right at the Hires junction, and completes a slow decline enveloped in forest sounds as it ends in the humid shade of an apple tree in a private corner of the nature center lawn.

Several other trails branch out from the visitor center, allowing hikers to investigate den trees, ferns, and modest views. For more options, stop near the sugar house for river loop, hemlock swamp, or beaver pond investigations. Sugar house parking is directly off Huntington Road 0.1 mile north of its junction with Sherman Hollow Road.

29 MOUNT INDEPENDENCE, ORANGE TRAIL

General description:	A walking tour of the site of a Revolutionary War fortification.
General location:	About 22 miles northwest of Rutland near the shore of Lake Champlain.
Length:	2.75 miles.
Difficulty:	Easy.
Elevation gain:	200 feet.
Special attractions:	Historic artifacts with views of Fort Ticonderoga and Lake Champlain.
Maps:	Handout maps are available at the trailhead; also USGS Ticonderoga quad.
For more information:	Chimney Point State Historic Site, RR 1, Box 3546, Vergennes, VT 05491; (802) 759-2412.

Finding the trailhead: From Vermont Highway 22A near Orwell, turn west onto Vermont Highway 73 following signs for Mount Independence Historic Sites. Bear left at the first fork after 0.4 mile and right 3 miles later. The road turns to gravel and parallels Lake Champlain before a final left

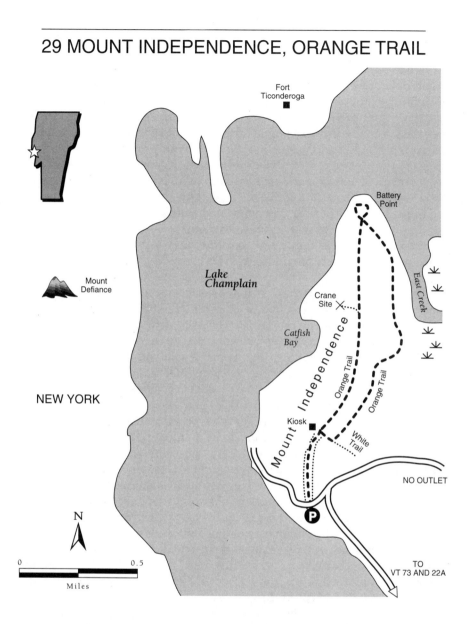

turn swings uphill past split-rail fences. A parking area is on the left directly across from the entrance gate 5.2 miles from VT 22A.

The hike: As war raged in the Champlain Valley more than two hundred years ago, Fort Ticonderoga was considered inadequate to stem a British advance. Additional fortifications were needed directly across the narrow lake that functioned as a ready made highway for invaders from Quebec. In the summer of 1776, on a high, flat promontory overlooking the marshes of

East Creek and the width of Lake Champlain, colonial Americans built Mount Independence, a star-shaped fort with horseshoe batteries that served a brief but stellar career.

The dual garrisons on Lake Champlain discouraged attacks until 1777, when both positions were overrun in a prologue to the American victory at Saratoga. Don't expect to see blockhouses or battlements, though, as you walk the site today. British soldiers burned Mount Independence when they left, within the year, and useful material was already salvaged by the turn of the eighteenth century. What you will see are fragments of stone foundations, traces of earthen parapets, sloping fields, regrown woods, Fort Ticonderoga, and the shore of Lake Champlain.

Hikers approach Mount Independence from the same direction as colonials did, on a wagon track running north from the access road. Of course our ancestors lacked the advantage of brochure maps now available at the entrance gate, or a kiosk providing trail information at the top of a breezy field.

Of the four trails that blanket this historic site, the Orange Trail is the principal route, coursing through fields of juniper and cedar, leading to Battery Point. Hikers follow a mowed swath to the right of the directory kiosk then turn left at a fork as the White Trail diverges right. Tracking north, the Orange Trail weaves through stands of maple and oak that were cleared in Revolutionary times, bisects a large meadow where the central stronghold stood, and detours left to a former crane site with views of Mount Defiance across the narrows of Lake Champlain.

While much of Battery Point is heavily wooded, the open tip where cannons stood still retains a commanding view of the slender lake that stretches north and the flag above Ticonderoga. An optional path trips down a short slope in front of the Horseshoe Battery and leads to a loop that's especially rewarding on a sweltering summer day. Amongst dragonflies and wildflower blooms, the old grade of a military road swoops down to Lake Champlain where a gently inclined bedrock platform eases away from shore. Splash in the shallows where Revolutionary soldiers built a floating bridge that linked Mount Independence with the allied fort still standing on the opposite shore.

After climbing back to Battery Point, bear left (west) to complete the Orange Trail, and then return through woods above East Creek overlooking a protective marsh. Interpretive signs mark historic remains of blockhouses and observation points as the trail reverses its course through juniper fields and blackberry thickets to conclude at the directory kiosk.

Mount Independence is open Wednesday through Sunday, Memorial Day through Columbus Day. No admission is charged.

General description:	A short nature walk to varied wetlands from the mouth of the LaPlatte River.
General location:	About 5 miles south of Burlington near the shore of Shelburne Bay.
Length:	1.3 miles round-trip.
Difficulty:	Easy.
Elevation gain:	Nominal.
Special attractions:	Diverse wetlands and migratory waterfowl.
Maps:	USGS Burlington quad.
For more information:	The Nature Conservancy, 27 State Street, Montpelier, VT 05602; (802) 229-4425.

Finding the trailhead: From the end of Interstate 189 at U.S. Highway 7 near Burlington, drive 2.9 miles south on Vermont Highway 7 and turn right onto Bay Road at a set of traffic lights. Cross the LaPlatte River on a small bridge after 1.1 mile and enter the Vermont Department of Fish and

A great blue heron in the shallows at LaPlatte River Marsh.

30 LAPLATTE RIVER MARSH NATURAL AREA

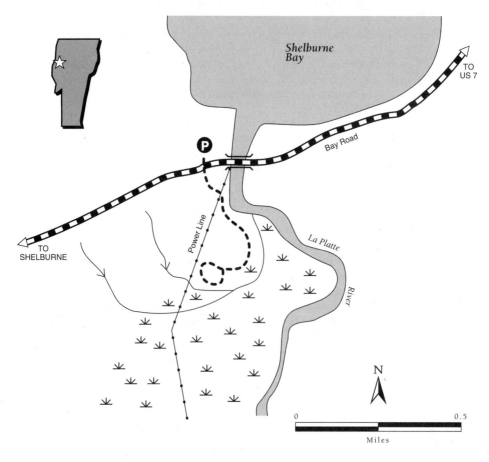

Wildlife parking lot, on the right just beyond the bridge. The trail is across the road near a sign placed by The Nature Conservancy.

The hike: Swamps are an acquired taste. The riverbanks, marshes, wooded wetlands, and duckweed-choked backwaters that abound in this natural area won't fit everyone's notion of "scenic," but hikers attuned to the ways of nature will find beauty in this trail. Birders intent on expanding their list of waterfowl should especially enjoy this path tracing a channel of the LaPlatte River from its mouth on Shelburne Bay.

Across the road from a fishing access parking area, a trampled path wends through the grass of a damp field, curls left under power lines, and enters thickets bordering the river on your left. Stepping off the trail and into the reeds along the bank, hikers hear bullfrogs croak and see kingfishers fly above a broad section of water not yet free of boating traffic. The path

Backwater channel, LaPlatte River Marsh.

curves away from the river as it slowly works upstream through pines and berry bushes only to return to shore to overlook billowing marshes filling a V where river channels divide.

A black-crowned heron may lift from the mud at your intrusion, and a great blue heron may stand like a statue in the shallow stream. Here, the river makes little pretense of maintaining a measurable flow. Threading south through woodlands of birch and pine, the trail maintains a 20-yard distance from wetlands that are now more settled marsh than moving stream. A cattail cove forces the path to hook sharply to the right, cross an elevated bridge, and circle back to the river before hikers find a registration box near the far end of the trail. Silver pickets of dead trees poke up from mats of bright green vegetation as the final loop turns its back on the sluggish river and returns to the outbound path near the bridge in the cattail cove.

For a change of pace, return to the parking lot and look about 100 yards farther up the road. The next driveway enters Shelburne Bay Park, where hiking trails skim to the top of Allen Hill and points on the open bay.

31 MISSISQUOI NATIONAL WILDLIFE REFUGE, BLACK AND MAQUAM CREEK TRAILS

General description:	A short nature walk by wetlands and creeks in the Missisquoi River delta.
General location:	30 miles north of Burlington.
Length:	2.2 miles.
Difficulty:	Easy.
Elevation gain:	Nominal.
Special attractions:	Wetlands and wildlife.
Maps:	Handout guides are available at the trailhead; also USGS East Alburg quad.
For more information:	Refuge Manager, Missisquoi National Wildlife Refuge, P.O. Box 163, Swanton, Vermont 05488-0163; (802) 868-4781.

Finding the trailhead: From Exit 21 off Interstate 89, follow Vermont Highway 78 west as it turns right at the village green and weaves through the town of Swanton. The headquarters of the Missisquoi National Wildlife Refuge are on the left, 3.6 miles from the interstate. Park near a kiosk behind the building.

The hike: Part of the Missisquoi River delta at the northern end of Lake Champlain, 6,338 acres of natural marshes, bulrush wetlands, open water, and wooded swamps make the Missisquoi National Wildlife Refuge a critical link in the Atlantic Flyway. Migratory birds, from wood ducks to war-

31 MISSISQUOI NATIONAL WILDLIFE REFUGE, BLACK AND MAQUAM CREEK TRAILS

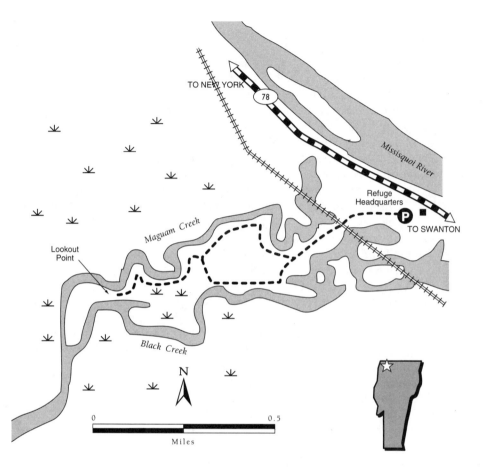

blers, commonly nest in this preserve, and multiple species of geese, herons, sandpipers and hawks pass through as seasonal visitors. Coyotes, river otters, and a host of small mammals also call this refuge home. For complete information on recreational opportunities and wildlife in the area, pick up one of the helpful brochures available at the trailhead.

Canoe routes explore many miles of the Missisquoi River and Dead Creek deltas, but wetland environments don't easily accommodate pedestrian travel. In this case, hikers are limited to a pair of trails wandering through wooded thickets that separate Black and Maquam creeks. Be forewarned—it's not what you expect. Think of coastal Virginia or the swamps of the south and you won't be far from the mark, though—ribbons of dark, motionless water winding through tangled vegetation, with the call of a bird or buzz of an insect piercing the afternoon. Patience is the primary tool of wildlife watchers in such places. Scattered benches at creekside overlooks help you perfect the art.

From a kiosk behind the refuge headquarters, a mowed swath angles through an open meadow, crosses an active railroad track, and passes several interpretive signs as it enters the dense woods. Thickets of fern, alder, and aspen border a woodcock management clearing as the path edges toward Black Creek, a languid flow of murky water dusted with yellow pollen. As uninviting as it sounds to humans, a maze of tracks on these muddy banks prove its appeal to other creatures.

Bear right at a nature trail sign pointing toward Maquam Creek and remain on the broad track that wends a crooked course along its wooded bank. Periodic beaver runs provide handy pathways to the water as a trail sprinkled with crushed stone twists its way to an observation bench near an oxbow at another junction. To the left, a 0.1-mile connector diverges toward Black Creek, while the trail along Maquam Creek continues 0.5-mile straight ahead to Lookout Point. Footing deteriorates beyond this junction as the root-bound trail narrows, the creek grows broader and deeper, the earth sags to become even wetter, and the route dwindles to a muddy point.

At the convergence of Black and Maquam creeks, hikers discover a more familiar wetland environment where aquatic plants slant away from a shallow shore, and a honking V of soaring geese adds emphasis overhead. The trail may be wet in the vicinity of Lookout Point in certain seasons, but it's also a great place to search for wildlife. Before retracing your steps back to the connector path, be sure to check the marsh on the left, the banks of the quiet streams, and several areas adjacent to nesting boxes.

The return link to Black Creek leads past gray birch, maples, and vernal pools before it meets the end of a bridge 0.2 mile from the starting point of the nature trail. Bearing east, an 80-yard boardwalk curls through seasonal wetlands as the Black Creek trail discloses one more variation on the delta environment. Here, floating mats of bright green duckweed blanket the water's surface, making a home for crustaceans and insects, a feast for waterfowl. This tranquil route ultimately ends as it began, reverting to a grass and crushed stone path that nudges away from the water and quietly wanders back to the trailhead.

Autumn stillness at Maquam Creek.

General description:	A barrier-free stroll on a drive-up summit suitable for any family.
General location:	13 miles south of Burlington.
Length:	0.25 mile.
Difficulty:	Easy.
Elevation gain:	Nominal.
Special attractions:	Picnic grounds with Lake Champlain and Adirondack views.
Maps:	Handout maps are available at the park; also USGS Mount Philo quad.
For more information:	Mount Philo State Park, RD 1, Box 1049, North Ferrisburg, VT 05473; (802) 425-2390.

Finding the trailhead: Mount Philo State Park is located east of U.S. Highway 7 about 13 miles south of Burlington. Turn east at blinker lights about 2.6 miles south of Charlotte or 1.2 miles north of North Ferrisburg. Stop at a crossroads after 0.6 mile, and the summit road to Mount Philo lies dead ahead. The contact station, parking lot, and trailhead are all at the top of the mountain, where a day-use fee is charged. The park is open from mid-May to early October.

The hike: Mount Philo brings back memories of those movies from my youth where daring explorers climbed a flat-topped mountain lost in prehis-

The Adirondacks and Champlain basin from the "island" of Mount Philo.

32 MOUNT PHILO STATE PARK

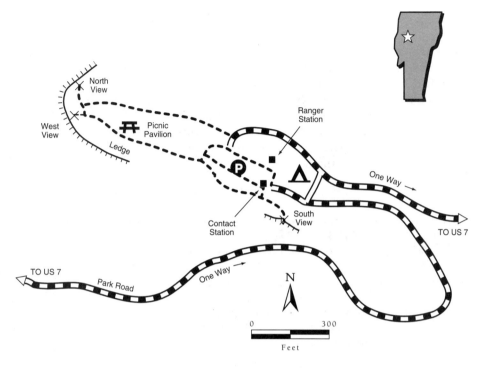

toric time. Not exactly *Jurassic Park*, but the same general idea. *Tyrannosaurus rex* doesn't live in Vermont, but visitors to Mount Philo ascend an ancient island, crossing gravel beaches that rimmed an arctic sea some 10,000 years ago. Just like the movies, this self-contained summit survives in a world of its own, but campgrounds, picnic areas, and magnificent Lake Champlain views stand in for giant monsters as entertainment suited to a family crowd.

There really isn't much hiking to be done at Mount Philo, although a few hardy folks trudge up the auto road. More to the point is laid-back enjoyment of fresh air and terrific views. Wooden tables rest in a series of clearings that line the parking lot. Step out of your car and you've already arrived at one of New England's most picturesque picnic spots. Towering almost 800 feet above the floor of the fertile valley, hikers can enjoy their lunch accompanied by southern views of a lowland region once submerged by Lake Vermont, a vast basin of glacial meltwater that rose 500 feet higher than the present shore of Lake Champlain.

Smooth paths and easy grades make most of this summit accessible to the entire family, with a picnic pavilion, restroom, and overnight lean-to that are all barrier free. For a short exploration, follow a gravel trail 100 yards west from the parking lot, pass the pavilion, and walk through a patch of lawn. Straight ahead, a dark red lump of quartzite rock supports a railing on the brink of a ledge with inspiring western views. To the right, a rougher path leads 90 yards downhill to a second lookout with impressive views that sweep even farther north. From either location, Lake Champlain isn't just a distant surface—it's a blue water superstar, a quivering platform for miles of Adirondack peaks in faraway New York. The observation point makes the lake seem close enough for hikers to examine details of farms and villages that line its eastern shore.

When you've had your fill of panoramas, retreat to the red rock ledge near the patch of pavilion lawn. Walk back the way you came or complete an easy (but not barrier-free) loop through wooded groves that returns to the exit driveway on the north side of the parking lot.

33 RED ROCKS PARK

General description:	A short promenade along the shore of Lake Champlain.
General location:	South Burlington.
Length:	1.2 miles round-trip.
Difficulty:	Easy.
Elevation gain:	100 feet.
Special attractions:	Picnic grounds, beach, and lakefront mountain views.
Maps:	USGS Burlington quad, or brochure available from the address below.
For more information:	South Burlington Recreation Department, 575 Dorset Street, South Burlington, VT 05403; (802) 658-7956.

Finding the trailhead: From the end of Interstate 189 at its junction with U.S. Highway 7, turn left (south) on US 7 then promptly turn right onto Queen City Park Road. Bear right at a stop sign onto Industrial Parkway, cross a one-lane bridge, and turn left onto Central Avenue within 0.6 mile. The entrance to Red Rocks Park is on the right in another 0.1 mile.

A day-use fee is charged for driving into the park, but hikers can leave their vehicles outside the gate and walk down a driveway that branches right. The trailhead is adjacent to a turnaround point by the lake.

The hike: Boats, beaches, Lake Champlain, Adirondack peaks, the Taconic Range, and a view of Camel's Hump that soars behind Shelburne Bay—not bad for an urban hike less than a mile from an interstate highway. In the grand tradition of genteel promenades, the wafting breezes and craggy shores

110

33 RED ROCKS PARK

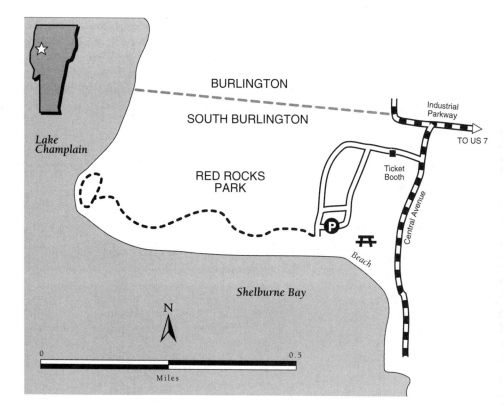

of this walk in Red Rocks Park dispense the perfect antidote to the stresses of city life.

A maze of paths wander through the tall pine forest that blankets Red Rocks Park, but this Lake Champlain walk begins at the end of the driveway loop where parking signs point to the left and trail signs to the right. Take the maintained path that branches north closest to the shore as it quickly rises in the shade of evergreens to a maple-covered knoll and the first outstanding view. Brushed by cedar trees, a deep red outcrop frames a unique perspective on Vermont. From here, sailboats appear to rock at anchor at the base of Camel's Hump.

Dipping down from the knoll, the trail quickly reaches more traditional Champlain views as hikers safely stroll behind a metal rail that arches above the water. This interlude is expressly made for leisurely observation of majestic mountain chains that flank the narrow lake as it fades into mist and sunlight to the south.

Alternate paths wander off in both directions, but the core of this lakeside trail eases to the right, advancing through a curlicue bend that descends to water level. Within splashing distance of the rockbound shore, the end of the trail coils back on itself amid crisp western views of fishing boats riding a gusty chop and a jagged horizon filled with the high peaks of New York.

As short as this walk may be, spacious picnic grounds above a sandy beach make Red Rocks Park a great destination on a summer day. You'll find picnic tables, fire grates, and a grassy lawn on the opposite branch of the driveway loop, all an easy walk from the trailhead.

34   SHAW MOUNTAIN NATURAL AREA

General description:	An afternoon walk to mountain and marsh in a preserve held by The Nature Conservancy.
General location:	About 20 miles northwest of Rutland.
Length:	2.4 miles round-trip.
Difficulty:	Moderate.
Elevation gain:	300 feet.
Special attractions:	Wildlife, wetlands, and diverse natural communities.
Maps:	USGS Benson quad or trail brochures available from the address below.
For more information:	The Nature Conservancy, 27 State Street, Montpelier, VT 05602; (802) 229-4425.

Finding the trailhead: About 7 miles north U.S. Highway 4, turn west off Vermont Highway 22A following signs for Benson and Benson Landing. Continue straight through the four-corner stop sign at the Benson Village Store, pass a cemetery, and turn left onto a gravel road 0.3 mile from the village. Take the first road to the right after another 0.5 mile, then continue 1.75 miles farther. Small signs from The Nature Conservancy appear on both sides of the road before a large Shaw Mountain Natural Area sign marks the trailhead on the left.

The hike: A limestone uplift rising high above ponds, marshes, and forests on the ancient seabed of the Champlain lowlands, Shaw Mountain harbors an astounding array of natural communities now preserved by The Nature Conservancy. Even if you don't know *Monotropa uniflora* (Indian pipe) from *Sanguinaria canadensis* (bloodroot), you can still enjoy the Shaw Mountain Natural Area. A handy trail guide identifies several unique plants for the uninitiated, but a springtime riot of blooming flowers, an oak-hickory summit forest, bobcat dens, stalking herons, and wild turkeys nesting at the peak provide familiar attractions that should motivate any hiker.

Wild ginger grows in moist forest soil where the white-blazed path snakes steeply to the top of a stony hill crowding the trailhead on the left. Shaded

34 SHAW MOUNTAIN NATURAL AREA

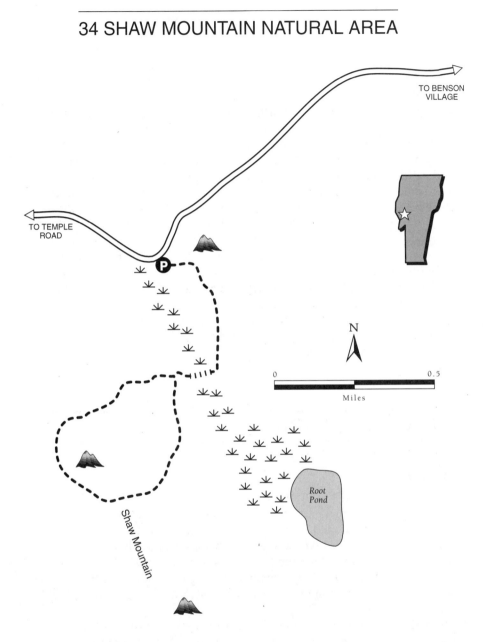

by tall oaks and maple trees, the trail passes a registration box on a smaller knoll and slowly begins a gradual descent down the backside of the ridge. Lost in a realm of grassy woods splotched by springtime sun, hikers ramble through sections of forest rich with abundant wildflowers and unique species of native plants. Wander into the woods for a clear view of Root Pond through the trees before the trail curls right and completes the descent, returning to its original elevation at a narrow neck of the marsh.

Step with care as you exit the forest and cross the wooden walkway spanning a cattail swamp. Herons often search the marsh, which fans out to the left, and the slightest movement chases frogs back to a pond that hides them, on the right. The ascent of Shaw Mountain begins immediately from the opposite shore of the marsh, where the trail swings briefly north a few yards above the tadpole pool, then twists left to climb 75 yards upslope. As the path meets the return leg of the circle around the summit, follow the arrows to the right to begin a counter-clockwise mountain loop.

The trek to the summit of Shaw Mountain is much more gradual than the hill climb near the trailhead, but here the forest floor is more typically covered by ferns and low-growing brush until almost the very top. As you enter open stands of oak-hickory forest that roll across the summit, scan the branches of surrounding trees and listen for telltale flaps or cackles that betray the presence of wild turkeys, and peek between leaves for hints of views that reach to Lake Champlain. Take a minute also to check out a shagbark hickory, a seldom-seen tree readily identified by the unkempt texture of its trunk.

Summit blazes are distinctive (white striped with blue), but you'll need to look carefully in several places to find the route of your return, especially if you wander off-trail to look for wildlife or elusive views. Stay alert near the end of the mountain loop—it's easy to miss the turn that leads back to the trailhead—and begin a second lap.

THE CONNECTICUT VALLEY

OVERVIEW

From Beecher Falls to Brattleboro, the graceful turns of the Connecticut River define Vermont's eastern boundary. Channeled through a classic glacial valley once widened by gouges of mile-thick ice and terraced by the flow of water, today's river abides in a sculptured landscape of rounded hills and fertile plains. An interstate highway now follows the course of the river for much of the valley's length, tracing the ancient route of native canoes and enduring as a high-speed corridor for traveling the length of the state.

For hikers, this winding valley is significant for its history of sheer resistance. From north to south, Mount Monadnock, Mount Ascutney, the Pinnacle at Wilgus State Park, Black Mountain, and the prominence at Fort Dummer all represent different forms of geologic monadnock. Cores of rock that defied the glacier's push, they stand above the carved terrain. From these high points, hikers can choose from a broad selection of Connecticut Valley views.

35 MOUNT ASCUTNEY, WEATHERSFIELD TRAIL

General description:	A half-day hike to a challenging peak on Vermont's eastern border.
General location:	About 20 miles south of White River Junction, just west of the Connecticut River.
Length:	5.8 miles round-trip.
Difficulty:	Intermediate.
Elevation gain:	2,100 feet.
Special attractions:	Waterfalls and spectacular views from a summit observation tower.
Maps:	USGS Mount Ascutney quad.
For more information:	Agency of Natural Resources, Department of Forests, Parks and Recreation, District I, RR 1, Box 33, North Springfield, VT 05150; (802) 886-2215.

Finding the trailhead: Depart Interstate 91 at Exit 8 and drive 3.1 miles west on Vermont Highway 131. With the mountain's bulk looming above you, turn right (north) onto the gravel Cascade Falls Road, then bear left after 0.1 mile onto High Meadow Road at a sign for Weathersfield Trail parking. High Meadow Rd. turns sharply right at a private driveway 0.3 mile later before it dead-ends at the trailhead.

The hike: Don't be fooled by the lumpish profile of Mount Ascutney; this hike is more challenging than it looks. As you approach the base of the Weathersfield Trail from the Connecticut Valley, a single radio tower stands atop a subordinate peak that hides a greater height and conceals a deep ravine between the trailhead and actual summit. This deceptive mountain is a classic monadnock, a core of resistant rock that persevered an Ice Age winter. Passing glaciers long ago scoured away foothills that would have eased your climb, leaving only illusive slopes that vault steeply to the top.

From the upper corner of the parking area, the Weathersfield Trail climbs a bank of wooden steps and follows a blue-blazed path through a parklike setting of young hardwoods, a canopy shading the forest floor. At the crest of the first obscure ridge, the moderate climb flattens in denser woods, dips briefly to cross a drainage, and briskly zigzags up the steepest sections of the lower slopes.

Only 0.4 mile from the trailhead, the path crosses the top of Little Cascade Falls, a grand name for this plunge of a tiny brook. But additional switchbacks soon transport hikers to more intriguing sights as the trail crosses a stream that exits the base of a flumelike gorge. Granite and wooden steps carry you 40 feet up and out of this rocky cleft where small oaks surround open ledges with views of checkered farmlands that stretch southwest to clustered Green Mountain peaks.

The pace of the hike relaxes for the next 0.5 mile as the trail slabs northwesterly on a roller-coaster line that separates a steeper slope below from a moderate contour above. After a series of outstanding outlooks from open granite faces, the trail dips slightly to pass below a slide of jagged rocks, then drops sharply to Cascade Falls, 1.2 miles from the trailhead.

Hikers expect to greet waterfalls by looking up at tumbling cascades. The Weathersfield Trail reverses the process, guiding visitors to a tranquil glade near the lip of an 80-foot waterfall. Mountain vistas skim the treetops from the edge of this precipice, but think carefully before trying to negotiate the dangerous, eroded paths that descend to more traditional views.

The main trail turns right (northeast), stays east of the brook, and commences the last 1.7 miles to the summit with an ascent of a moderate slope. A smooth path over the soft duff of stately evergreens stretches calf muscles as you near the constricted head of the watershed. You'll catch a glimpse of West Peak and the transmission towers on Ascutney's summit just before the trail descends to span the brook and veers up the other side of the ravine at a sharp left (northwest) turn near a sign for "Half-Way Brooks," a no-longer-accurate remnant held over from a former route.

The climb eases again at the top of a ridge that radiates from West Peak, where a 35-yard spur leads right to Gus's Lookout, a granite outcrop with superb views of the Connecticut Valley and Mount Monadnock 40 miles southeast. Turning away from this peaceful vista in the shadow of the mountain's summit, the main trail re-enters the woods, rises past glacial erratics, and curls up a rocky slope to the top of West Peak, a local hang-gliding hub. Two large clearings are outfitted as launch sites, complete with windsocks and wooden platform. Hikers who reach this site can also enjoy the bird's-eye view of a crossroads town.

A rapid descent from Mount Ascutney.

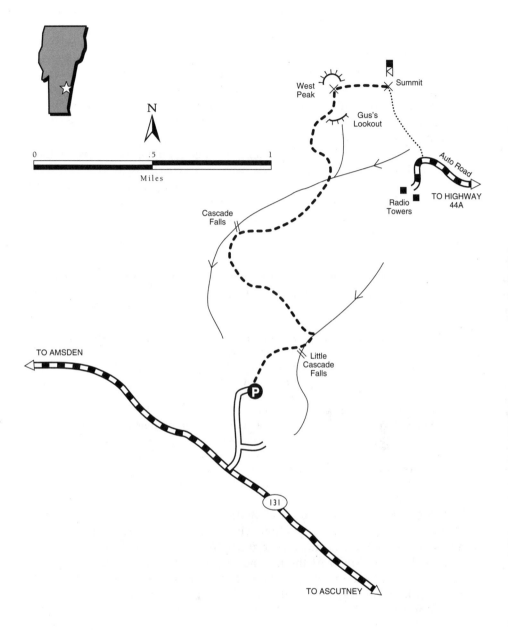

N

Miles

0 .5 1

West
Peak

Gus's
Lookout

Summit

Auto Road

TO HIGHWAY
44A

Radio
Towers

Cascade
Falls

TO AMSDEN

Little
Cascade
Falls

P

131

TO ASCUTNEY

A narrow path completes the ascent, ranging 0.2 mile east to the highest point on Mount Ascutney, where the Weathersfield Trail intersects a white-blazed path leading up from an auto road. About 80 yards to the right are two large transmission towers. About 50 yards to the left is the preferred destination, an observation tower with stunning 360-degree views. From the top of the tower, a mountainous collage sweeps the skyline of central Vermont, where ski trails carved on wooded slopes identify Stratton, Bromley, Okemo, Mount Snow, and Killington Peak. Across the shallow valley of the Connecticut River, the spine of the Monadnock-Sunapee Greenway inter-rupts the view to the east, while the White Mountains of northern New Hampshire add bumps to the far horizon.

For an easier approach, hikers can join hang-gliding aficionados by mak-ing use of the auto road that departs from Vermont Highway 44A at Mount Ascutney State Park, 1.1 mile west of U.S. Highway 5, north of Ascutney Village. A short loop to the observation tower and West Peak is possible by following the summit, Weathersfield, and hang-glider access trails.

36 BLACK MOUNTAIN NATURAL AREA

General description:	A short, energetic family hike to a backcountry peak that's close to town.
General location:	5 miles north of Brattleboro.
Length:	2.3 miles round-trip.
Difficulty:	Moderate.
Elevation gain:	1,000 feet.
Special attractions:	Pitch pine and scrub oak barrens with river and mountain views.
Map:	USGS Newfane quad.
For more information:	The Nature Conservancy, 27 State Street, Montpelier, VT 05602; (802) 229-4425.

Finding the trailhead: From Exit 3 off Interstate 89, travel 2 miles south on U.S. Highway 5 to its junction with Vermont Highway 30. Drive 5.1 miles north on VT 30, and turn right onto a green, one-lane bridge that crosses the West River. At the far end of the bridge, turn right again onto Rice Farm Road and watch for yellow Nature Conservancy signs. About 0.5 mile south of the bridge, a small driveway angles to the top of an embank-ment and trailhead parking on the left.

The hike: From the banks of the West River to the summit of Black Moun-tain, this undiscovered family hike conveys a sense of wildness just a few miles out of town. Don't expect an easy effort, though. Managed by The Nature Conservancy, this extraordinary preserve challenges your condition-ing on a bona fide mountain trail. On any given day, wildlife, views, and an

36 BLACK MOUNTAIN NATURAL AREA

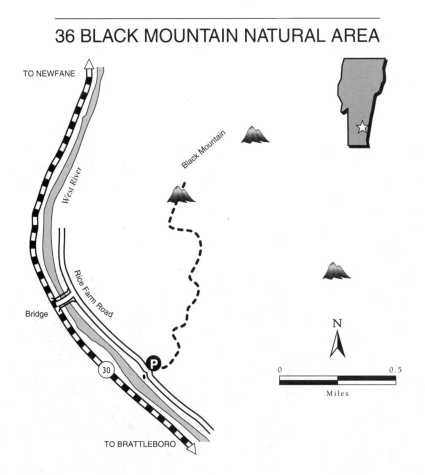

uncommon aura await hikers on this peak, but schedule a visit during blueberry season or when mountain laurel blooms and you'll have the chance to experience a special outdoor treat.

Before heading up the mountain, drop down the embankment on the opposite side of the road and check out 1,200 feet of brushy West River frontage. Botanists might spot a few rare species along the shore, but most hikers simply enjoy watching goldfinches on the wing or tiptoeing across the dry-topped stones that dot the summer stream.

A Nature Conservancy sign greets hikers about 100 yards up the gravel drive that angles easterly from the road. Curling right behind the trailhead, a woods road slices 75 yards farther up the slope, levels on a shady plateau, and swings left again through a blueberry swath parallel to a crude stone wall. At the end of the swath, the white-blazed trail departs the logging road, dips across a wetland on wooden planks, and finds a registration box before turning sharply left into ferns and fireweed.

An abrupt right turn around a gigantic maple tree aims the trail more

West River views adorn the summit of Black Mountain.

directly up the mountain, twisting, turning, and curling between boulders massed on the moderate slope. Marked by double blazes, a second sudden swerve then steers the trail left into glades of maple and oak as the path skirts a large clearing and glimpses the arch of the summit ahead. Keep a sharp eye on the blazes when the trail re-enters these spacious woods, weaving among huge beech and glacial erratics as it braves the bulk of the spirited climb.

You'll think the summit is near when the trail turns left and follows a contour at the base of a rock slab. Gentle breezes and sun-dappled views of hills beyond the West River contribute to the happy delusion, but hikers won't reach the end of this extended top until mountain laurel overwhelms the path and blueberries appear in quantities sufficient to fuel a feast.

Surrounded by flat islands of granite, pitch pine, and low scrub oak, the trail skims 60 yards below the actual peak, misses a few antennae at the very top, and begins a dead-end jaunt down the other side. Instead of following this last part, scamper off the trail and onto slanting ledge to meander about the mountain, absorb the atmosphere, and scope out the marvelous views. Mount Monadnock hovers on the skyline of New Hampshire to the east, far behind the sheer rock faces that gleam on a neighboring peak. Contained within this framework is the most distinctive view of all—the gentle hills that taper east along the West River Valley and meld with the plain of the Connecticut River at their junction in Brattleboro.

37 FORT DUMMER STATE PARK, SUNRISE TRAIL

General description:	A brief hilltop loop overlooking the Connecticut River; also a convenient campground with a barrier-free Adirondack shelter.
General location:	Immediately south of Brattleboro.
Length:	1.2 miles.
Difficulty:	Easy.
Elevation gain:	200 feet.
Special attractions:	Oak forests and Connecticut Valley views.
Maps:	Handout maps are available at the ranger station, or from the address below.
For more information:	Fort Dummer State Park, 434 Old Guilford Road, Brattleboro, VT 05301-3653; (802) 254-2610.

Finding the trailhead: From Exit 1 off Interstate 91, drive 0.35 mile north on U.S. Highway 5 and turn right onto Fairground Road. Turn right again after 0.5 mile onto South Main Street and continue straight ahead. The name of the street changes to Old Guilford Road before it dead-ends at the entrance to Fort Dummer State Park.

A day-use fee is collected at the ranger station. Drive uphill on the park

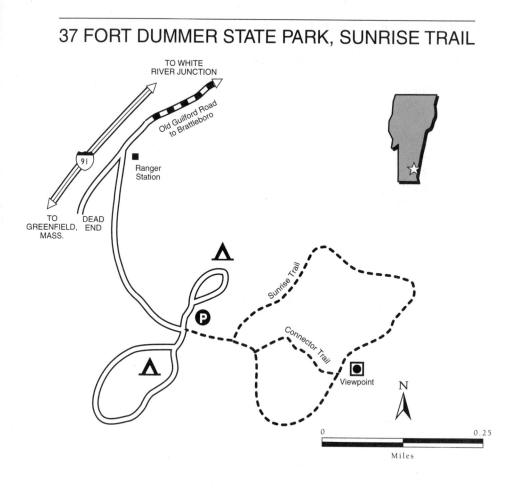

TO WHITE
RIVER JUNCTION

Old Guilford Road
to Brattleboro

91

Ranger
Station

TO
GREENFIELD,
MASS.

DEAD
END

Sunrise Trail

Connector Trail

P

Viewpoint

N

0   0.25

Miles

driveway to a junction with campground roads. The trailhead is on the east side of the junction.

The hike: A stone's throw from Interstate 91, not far from a fast-food zone, Fort Dummer once stood on the brink of the American frontier. Strategically built on the banks of the Connecticut River in 1724, the log fort was the first permanent white settlement in what later became Vermont, a link in the British defenses against French and Indian attack. Today no trace of the fortification remains. The original site was flooded when a dam was completed in 1908, but the present state park occupies a hill just south of Brattleboro that overlooks a still verdant slice of this historic river valley.

Hikers aren't drawn to this trail from far and wide, but it's a satisfying local walk and good recreation for campers spending the night in this well-maintained, easy access park. A broad path blazed in blue leads east from the campground road as the Sunrise Trail passes under hearty oaks and bears left at a signed junction after approximately 100 yards. Descending gently through glades of hemlock and pine, the path swings more distinctly north to begin its looping course. Signs on trees identify various species along the route. Vegetation here is more typical of southern New England with a wealth of oaks to feed red squirrels, deer, and wild turkeys. Interspersed at lower elevations are plentiful evergreens with needles that fall like rain in the gentle breeze of a summer afternoon.

Making its way east toward the river, the path turns right at the top of a gradual hill, sinks through a ferny hollow on wooden planks, and climbs easily again to reach a hardwood forest. A trail sign at the next corner directs hikers to follow the main route, which rises steadily to the height of land and even slopes down a bit before pausing at a convenient bench waiting by the side of the trail. Here, you may appreciate at leisure a long, narrow vista that highlights the meandering course of the Connecticut River and the summits of Massachusetts that roll off to the south.

Just beyond the overlook, the Connector Trail zips down a shortcut to the right, while the Sunrise Trail billows south on a gradual course that departs the top of the knoll. Both paths meet again in the bottom of a hollow as they jointly complete the loop and rise to the initial junction, 100 yards east of the campground road.

Hikers and campers should note that Fort Dummer State Park is only open seasonally, from mid-May to Labor Day. Check with the park for specific dates from year to year.

38 MOUNT MONADNOCK

General description:	A half-day hike from the Connecticut River to the top of Mount Monadnock.
General location:	Extreme northeastern Vermont.
Length:	4.5 miles round-trip.
Difficulty:	Intermediate.
Elevation gain:	2,100 feet.
Special attractions:	Wildlife, an invigorating climb, but (at present) no summit view.
Maps:	USGS Monadnock Mountain VT-NH quad.
For more information:	None available.

Finding the trailhead: Vermont Highway 102 parallels the Connecticut River between U.S. Highway 2 and the Canadian border. Park on the east side of VT 102 just south of the bridge that carries Vermont Highway 26 across the river to Colebrook, New Hampshire. The trailhead is on the west side of the road, about 70 yards south of the bridge.

The hike: Tell friends in southern Vermont that you walked from the Connecticut River to the top of Mount Monadnock, returned in the same day,

38 MOUNT MONADNOCK

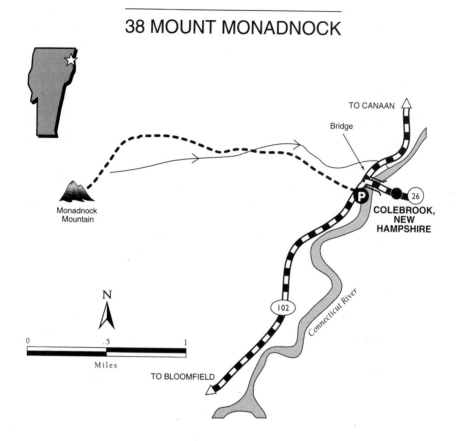

TO CANAAN

Bridge

Monadnock
Mountain

P

26

**COLEBROOK,
NEW
HAMPSHIRE**

N

0   .5   1

Miles

102

Connecticut River

TO BLOOMFIELD

and still made it home for dinner. No one will ever believe you, but complete this hike and you'll be telling the absolute truth. Of course, I'm not describing the famous Mount Monadnock that's 40 miles east of the river in extreme southwestern New Hampshire, but the unknown version close to the stream in far northeastern Vermont.

Geologically related by a common history of glaciation and only 25 feet different in height, the two Mounts Monadnock are otherwise quite distinct. Unlike its southern cousin, the northern rendition sprouts evergreens from its top, boasts no natural views, and appeals mostly for the simple pleasures of a stimulating hike. Still, forests, streams, and resident grouse are the basics of a woodland stroll, and it's possible that in the future this mountain might offer more. A summit tower is presently closed for lack of repairs. If it ever reopens, this peak will once again astonish hikers with sensational northern views.

Before hitting the trail, walk down a footpath on the banks of the river and dabble your toe in the stream. (It's a great way to embellish that story your friends will never believe.) Mission accomplished, cross the highway onto a private road that curls between two houses just north of a small

Columbia Bridge spans the Connecticut River

power line. This gravel road enters the woods after approximately 200 yards, rises through a corridor of young fir trees, and passes to the right of a small clearing that holds a stone foundation. Dwindling to a less traveled track where a sign now signifies "Trail," the route edges a ridge that falls off to the right and proceeds about 0.4 mile before the course narrows to a condition that matches the message of the sign.

Traces of a former access road remain evident for much of the hike. As a deep cleft that channels a stream converges from the right, the path crosses a log bridge close to a 6-foot falls. Ascending over rougher footing at a less aggressive pace, the trail angles south and west while it climbs a dominant ridge. After a session of sunny intervals between mature, well-spaced maples, the route sweeps to the right away from the brook's ravine and again climbs briskly on a loose rock trail slanting up the slope. Finally narrowed to a forest path, the end of the trail gains the upper ridge and traipses moderately along its shoulder to the base of the summit tower.

"No trespassing" signs and missing stairs prevent access to the tower that hoards unseen views of Camel's Hump, Mount Washington, and great chunks of Quebec. Happily, there are other ways to find contentment on this wooded peak. I unpacked my lunch in a quiet corner and played peekaboo with a spruce grouse plainly accustomed to having this summit to herself.

39 WILGUS STATE PARK, THE PINNACLE

General description:	A refreshing, 1-hour riverview walk only minutes from an interstate highway.
General location:	About 22 miles south of White River Junction near the banks of the Connecticut River.
Length:	1 mile round-trip to the summit, or an optional 1.2-mile loop.
Difficulty:	Moderate, but with easy options.
Elevation gain:	300 feet.
Special attractions:	Campsites, picnic grounds, riverbank strolls, and views of the Connecticut Valley.
Maps:	USGS Mount Ascutney quad.
For more information:	Agency of Natural Resources, Department of Forests, Parks and Recreation, District I, RR 1, Box 33, North Springfield, VT 05150; (802) 886-2215.

Finding the trailhead: Depart Interstate 91 at Exit 8 (Ascutney) and follow Vermont Highway 131 east 0.4 mile to its junction with U.S. Highway 5. Turn right on US 5 and drive south 1.1 miles to a small trail sign on the right (west) side of the road directly opposite the Wilgus State Park office. Park off the east side of the highway without blocking the gate, enter the park and check with the ranger on duty, or continue another 0.2 mile south to a large gravel turnout that accommodates additional parking.

The hike: Cruising the eastern flank of the Green Mountain State on I-91, most drivers catch only fleeting glimpses of the broad Connecticut River. Masked by hills and bits of forest flashing by at highway speeds, pastoral scenes along the tranquil river remain elusive though close at hand. For travelers who would like to stretch their legs, gain an overview of the valley, or simply relax on grassy banks that line the peaceful stream, Wilgus State Park conveniently waits only 1.5 miles from the highway.

While the name The Pinnacle conjures images of stone towers and harrowing climbs, technical gear is hardly necessary to complete this simple walk to a small prominence that overlooks a slice of the Connecticut Valley. Railroad ties step up an embankment at the edge of US 5, as blue-blazed pine trees mark a trail that runs north parallel to the road for about 100 yards. Turning sharply back on itself and crossing the face of the angular slope, the broad duff-covered path rapidly levels to find itself south of the starting point but high above the road.

After a second brief ascent, the easy trail curls right and serpentines through a stand of conifers to a signed junction 0.2 mile from the summit. Bear right at the junction and descend a few steps until the well-marked path narrows, curves to the left, and swings upward at the obscure crossing of an old woods road. With the aid of several natural stone steps, a moderate 150-yard climb conquers the steepest part of the hill before the trail

126

39 WILGUS STATE PARK, THE PINNACLE

TO ASCUTNEY
Power Line
VERMONT
WILGUS STATE PARK
NEW HAMPSHIRE
Park Boundary
Park HQ
US 5
Connecticut River
N
0
0.5
Miles
TO BELLOWS FALLS

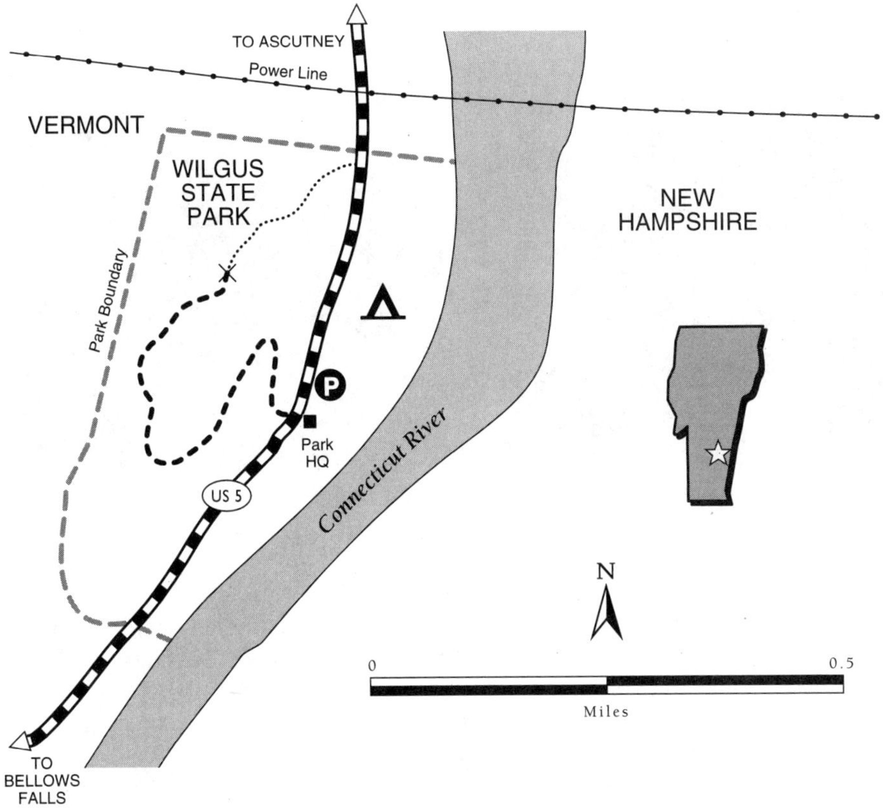

comfortably winds north to an overlook about 30 yards shy of the wooded summit. Maples, birch, oak, and pine furnish shade for the close-cropped view. Across the dark river water, evergreen slopes tumble down the distant shore, verdant pastures rise on rolling hills, and the tops of New Hampshire mountains recall greater heights beyond.

Once atop the summit, most hikers simply retrace their steps and return the way they came. If you're not put off by steeper slopes or a walk on a narrow road, the trail completes a loop by continuing over the summit and rapidly descending the other side. Watch carefully after dropping about 0.1 mile from the top, where a tricky turn bears right instead of following the crest of a falling ridge. The extended trail rejoins the highway 0.3 mile north of where you began. Across the way, a faint path returns through the campground and park, a long but sensible route that avoids danger on the busy road.

Only in a literal sense is The Pinnacle the high point of Wilgus State Park.

The Connecticut River, placid eastern border of Vermont.

Other great recreation waits for visitors who officially pass through the gate. Picnic, fish, launch a canoe, camp in lean-tos under the pines, stroll in luxury on grassy banks above the placid stream, or watch the life of the river glide by from a bench in the morning sun. Given a chance, there's plenty here to encourage a longer stay.

THE HIGH FIVE

OVERVIEW

The Appalachian Mountain Club has long maintained an official list of summits in Maine, New Hampshire, and Vermont that qualify hikers for membership in the New England Four Thousand Footer Club. The five mountains grouped in this section represent not a geographic region, but the Vermont summits eligible for inclusion on this elite New England list.

Hikers not yet familiar with this state are often surprised to learn that nearly 70 miles of mountainous ridge separate Mount Mansfield from Killington Peak, and that only two of Vermont's five highest summits are contained within Green Mountain National Forest. Each of these magnificent mountains rises to sensational 360-degree views, and three (Mount Mansfield, Camel's Hump, and Abraham) support communities of rare and endangered arctic plants not otherwise found in the state of Vermont. These trails, then, are grouped not to encourage "peak-bagging" competition, but for convenient reference to the special pleasures of these scattered alpine hikes.

40   MOUNT MANSFIELD, SUNSET RIDGE TRAIL

General description:	A classic ascent of a rocky ridge to the highest peak in Vermont.
General location:	About 17 miles east of Burlington and 22 miles northwest of Montpelier.
Length:	6.6 miles round-trip.
Difficulty:	Difficult.
Elevation gain:	2,500 feet.
Special attractions:	Rare alpine plants and flowers; magnificent summit views.
Maps:	USGS Mount Mansfield quad.
For more information:	Department of Forests, Parks and Recreation, District IV, 324 North Main Street, Barre, VT 05641; (802) 479-3241.

Finding the trailhead: Driving east from Jericho on Vermont Highway 15, bear right at a fork onto Steam Mill Road following signs to Underhill Center. From a stop sign in the center of the village continue 1 mile straight through town and turn right onto Mountain Road. The entrance to Underhill State Park, a toll house, and trailhead parking are 2.7 miles up the road.

The hike: Sprawled across the massive bulk of the highest peak in Vermont, the crest of Mount Mansfield is said to resemble the profile of a human face. From the Forehead in the south to the Adam's Apple in the north, assorted portions of this bumptious summit have been named for body parts. Once you know that the Chin is the highest point, the Nose hosts an auto road, and the Long Trail (LT) connects them all, maps and descriptions of hikes on this mountain make a lot more sense.

Of course, facial analogies don't really do justice to a premier New England peak. Immersed in exquisite mountain scenes, the 2-mile walk from Forehead to Chin traverses a National Natural Landmark and the largest expanse of arctic vegetation to be found in the State of Vermont. Whether hiking from the base, scrambling up from the gondola, or strolling over from the auto road, crowds of visitors flock to this mountain to relish the sumptuous views and the vast acres of alpine flowers that blanket this special peak. In all the excitement, just remember the basic rules: Be alert for changes in weather, and do your part to protect this fragile environment by staying on the trail.

129

40 MOUNT MANSFIELD, SUNSET RIDGE TRAIL

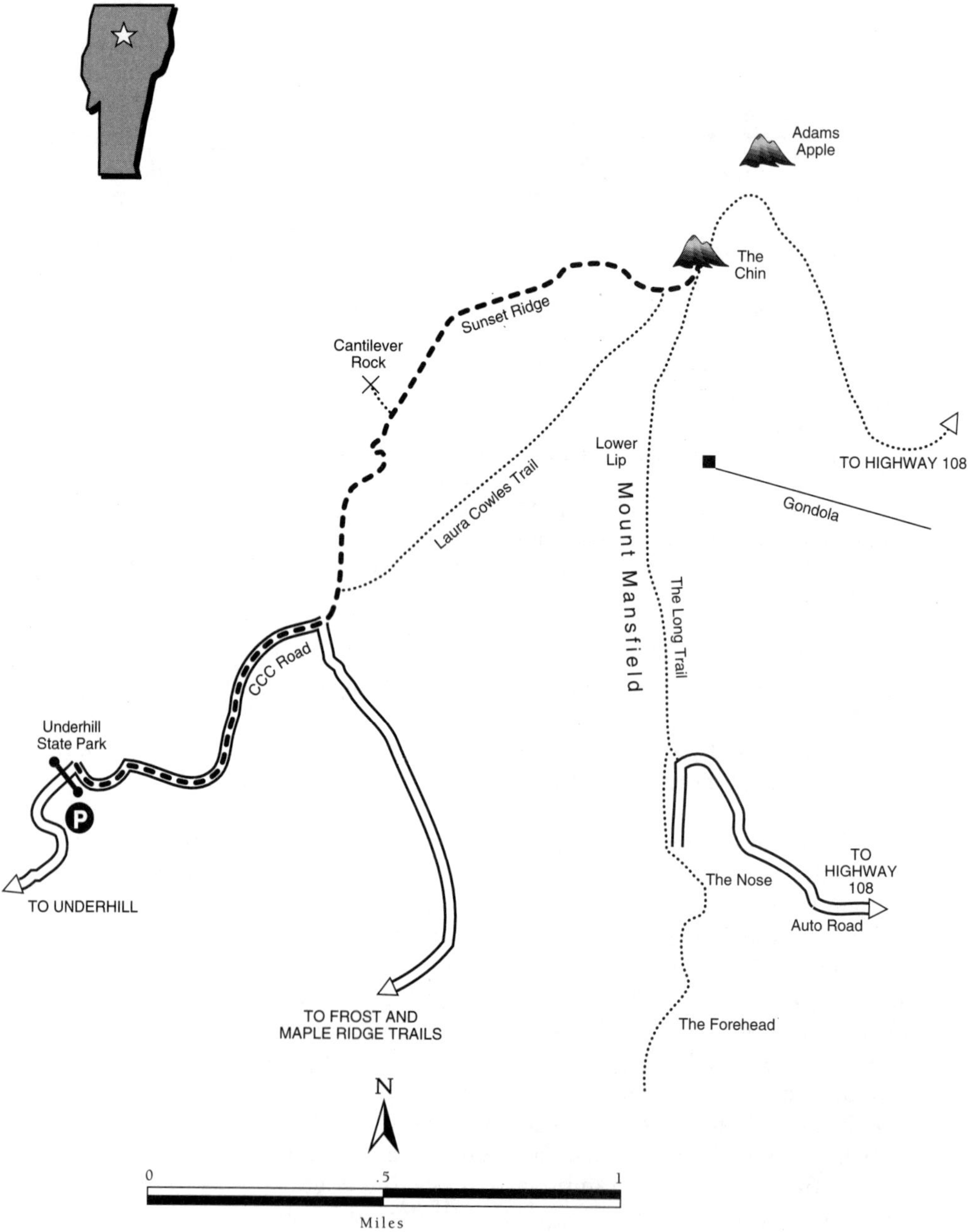

Adams Apple
The Chin
Sunset Ridge
Cantilever Rock
Lower Lip
TO HIGHWAY 108
Gondola
Laura Cowles Trail
Mount Mansfield
The Long Trail
CCC Road
Underhill State Park
P
TO UNDERHILL
The Nose
TO HIGHWAY 108
Auto Road
TO FROST AND MAPLE RIDGE TRAILS
The Forehead
N
0
.5
1
Miles

Traveling east from Burlington on Interstate 89, hikers see the face of Mount Mansfield standing in proud relief. But those with a yen for mountain travel also notice something else. A flying buttress of bright gray rock supports the massive Chin, a dogleg ridge extending west and erupting from a verdant forest that cloaks a glacial cirque. The vision is Sunset Ridge, a classic New England hike complete with hardy boulder scrambles and winds that can, on occasion, peel a wool cap off your head.

From a gate near the parking lot in Underhill State Park, a gravel Civilian Conservation Corps (CCC) road climbs briskly for about 1 mile to a turnaround loop at a sharp right turn. To the left, the trail to Sunset Ridge immediately steps over a wooden bridge 0.7 mile from Cantilever Rock, 2.2 miles from Mansfield's Chin. Spanning two more brooks within the next 100 yards, the blue-blazed path bears left as it intersects the bottom of the Laura Cowles Trail at yet another crossing. Rocks and streams abound on this moderate climb, but boulder steps and plank bridges ease the way. By the time the path reaches the spur to Cantilever Rock, the trail soars high enough to enjoy southwestern views from a handy bench that waits at the scenic junction. Rest for a minute, but don't pass up a short detour on this rugged spur that leads to a 30-foot monolith jutting from the face of a barren cliff.

Birch trees and shrunken evergreens filter the sunlight, as the route clambers over jumbles of boulders and short pitches of slab to the lower end of Sunset Ridge, where a bulbous outcrop opens views of Mansfield's western cheek. Ducking back under cover, the trail generates handhold scrambles and difficult footing as it pops rapidly higher. A rib of gleaming rock at last

Mount Mansfield from Nose to Chin, a classic Long Trail hike.

greets hikers with a panoramic scene from the top of New York's Mount Marcy to the tip of Mount Mansfield's Nose.

A sheltered col grants hikers final brief protection as the trail climbs briskly above timberline into a zone of arctic plants and weather. Cairns supplement blue-painted blazes on the windblown slopes of this austere flank. Off to the right, Maple Ridge comes into its own as the southern brace for the summit's head. Struggling upward, searching in vain for sight of the highest peak, hikers slowly comprehend a shocking truth—Mansfield has a double chin! From the junction with the Story Trail 0.2 mile from the LT and 0.4 mile from the peak, the extra bulge of West Chin blocks the summit view. Bearing right and angling slowly around the contour of this added lump, the Sunset Ridge Trail eases past the top of the Laura Cowles Trail, curls left, and ends 100 yards later at the Long Trail junction, about halfway between the Chin and Lower Lip.

To your left, sedges, mosses, Labrador tea, and selections of alpine berries line the path that runs north to the top of the Chin where islands in Lake Champlain compete with the Worcester Range for the prize of outstanding view. My picks are the precipitous look into the depths of Smugglers Notch, or the long view down the Mansfield ridge to the Green Mountains stretching south.

To your right, the LT explores the rest of Mansfield's summit, a mountain playground that's hard to resist if you're blessed with decent weather. Be prepared for a bit of an effort, though. A traverse of this alpine ridge gains and loses hundreds of feet in very rapid order. If you don't make it to the Nose, at least check out the lower lip with its knee-wobbling views from unforgiving cliffs and a completely novel perspective on the climb to the rugged Chin.

The Laura Cowles Trail is an alternate route back to the CCC road. It's consistently steep and marginally shorter but lacks ridgeline views. Dropping off the headwall midcirque and plunging past woods and streams, this rough path is plagued with lots of runoff, but it's quicker to head to high cover and provides generally better traction. It's a route to consider for rapid escape if the weather threatens to make a descent on Sunset Ridge a hazardous proposition.

General description:	A 5- to 6-hour round-trip to the second highest summit in Vermont.
General location:	About 7 miles east of Rutland.
Length:	7 miles round trip.
Difficulty:	Intermediate.
Elevation gain:	2,500 feet.
Special attractions:	Three-state views of the Green Mountains, White Mountains, Taconic Range, and Adirondacks.
Maps:	USGS Killington Peak, Pico Peak, and Rutland quads.
For more information:	None available.

Finding the trailhead: From the junction of U.S. Highways 4 and 7 in Rutland, travel 5 miles east on US 4 and turn right onto Wheelerville Road. This narrow byway tracks south through the watershed for the City of Rutland, makes several stream crossings, and passes a number of private homes before reaching a small turnout 3.9 miles from the highway. When the road ahead turns sharply right and a gate stands directly before you, the turnout and trailhead are immediately to your left.

The hike: Second in stature only to Mount Mansfield and many miles south of Vermont's other 4,000-foot summits, Killington Peak is well positioned to attract plenty of hiking action. Home to one of the largest ski areas in the east, this summit also features mountain biking, active chairlifts, and bustling tourism even in summer. For hikers who'd like to climb this mountain but escape the crush of visitors to the U.S. Highway 4 corridor, the Bucklin Trail offers a serene backwoods experience until the very top, where reminders of development pale in comparison to the pleasures of remarkable views.

Bearing east from the parking turnout, the Bucklin Trail departs on a blue-blazed woods road that penetrates a stand of pine crisscrossed by skid road paths. The murmur of a brook signals a slick stone crossing after about 0.15 mile; before the road narrows, ferns and violets crowd the trail, and the sight of a stream fades in and out on the right. After a snowmobile track makes an entrance across a collapsed logging bridge, the path regains a woods road look and maintains its steady progress into the watershed. A mile or so from the trailhead, the route turns right in the middle of a tiny clearing, scampers down an embankment, and skips to the far side of the stream.

With the sound of water now bubbling on the left, trees overarch a wildflower-covered path that doubles the distance already gained along the brook. At a well-marked divergence a little more than halfway to the peak, the carefree advance rapidly ends as the route steps up to the right and takes its

41 KILLINGTON PEAK, BUCKLIN TRAIL

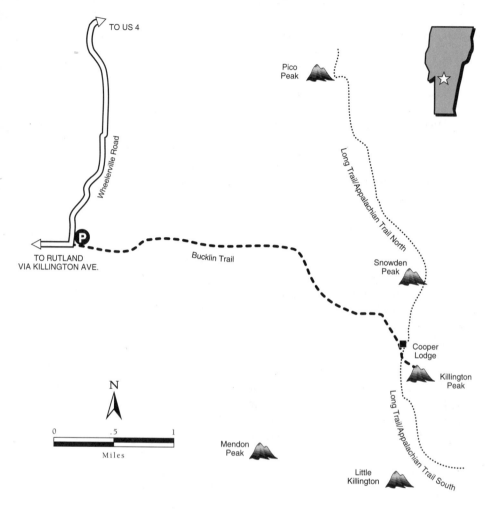

leave of the woods road that continues ahead. No longer a logging track, the trail remains broad and affords reliable footing as it eagerly commences a crisp ascent of the mountain's steepening slope.

Pico Peak appears to the north during a persistent 0.75-mile climb, but a lowering skyline behind trees ahead holds the promise of an effort that's less demanding. Evergreens catch the breeze on the upper slopes as the trail joins a water spur path within sight of Cooper Lodge, a backpacker's shelter barely visible 50 yards to the left where the Bucklin Trail ends at the Long Trail/Appalachian Trail (LT/AT) junction.

Cooper Lodge is a crude, well-worn shelter that no doubt looks more inviting when you're caught in a raging storm. I prefer the tent platform located a little south (right, uphill) on the LT/AT, where hikers to Killington Peak also find the blue-blazed spur to the top. This steep, rocky, 0.2-mile diversion charts a tricky course to Killington's granite crown, where radio antennae and a fire tower that's closed to the public hunch below the open peak.

The vistas from this summit are absolutely astounding—or so I've been told. My visits seem to occur in the gloaming, when scudding clouds turn chairlifts ghostly in the col between Killington and Pico Peak. The tallest summits often capture passing clouds. Don't be surprised by misty views. If you are blessed with clear blue skies, the full cast of the Green Mountains spread before you north and south, hazy forms of the White Mountains cap horizons to the east, and the Taconic Range, Lake Champlain, and the distant Adirondacks line up in ranked formations receding to the west. Allow plenty of time to savor these scenes from the lee of a rocky crag before retracing the steps that return you to the bottom of this backside trail.

42 MOUNT ELLEN, JERUSALEM TRAIL

General description:	A roundabout day hike to the third highest peak in Vermont.
General location:	17 miles southwest of Montpelier.
Length:	8.6 miles round-trip.
Difficulty:	Intermediate.
Elevation gain:	2,500 feet.
Special attractions:	Spectacular Green Mountain views.
Maps:	USGS Mount Ellen quad.
For more information:	Middlebury Ranger District, Route 7, RR 4, Box 1260, Middlebury, VT 05753; (802) 388-4362.

Finding the trailhead: Vermont Highway 17 runs east/west on a looping course from Vermont Highway 116 north of Bristol to Vermont Highway 100 just south of Waitsfield. Turn south off VT 17 onto a gravel road 3.6 miles east of VT 116, just beyond a country store. Bear left onto Jerusalem Road, turn left again after 0.8 mile onto Jim Dwire Road, and look for the trail on the right in another 0.5 mile. Park off the side of the road or in a small clearing about 50 yards south of a sign that marks the trailhead.

The hike: Clusters of steep-sided hills and hollows make this region near Appalachian Gap one of the roughest in the Green Mountain State. Though a skier's chairlift shoots straight to the top of the third highest peak in Vermont, hikers intent on conquering Mount Ellen must employ more indirect means. In the 16 miles between Cooley Glen (see Hike 19) and VT 17, only two routes intercept the Long Trail (LT) ridge, a set of parallel paths that obliquely approach opposite ends of Lincoln Mountain. While the Battell Trail (see Hike 44) aims just below Mount Abraham, Lincoln's anchoring summit to the south, the Jerusalem Trail arcs well to the north, giving hikers a roundabout path that connects to the top of Mount Ellen, Lincoln Mountain's tallest peak.

The first 2.5 miles of this hike are uneventful. Thick woods extend to the edge of the gravel road where a small sign and a break in the ferns identify the Jerusalem trailhead. Crossing a small brook within 50 yards, the narrow dirt track spans a number of drainages as it sets a steady pace pursuing its uphill trek. The last 0.5 mile to the crest of the ridge requires more intense effort, but the gradual escalation never exceeds a moderate pitch.

The Jerusalem Trail ends at the LT junction. To the left, it's 3.5 miles to Appalachian Gap, 0.4 mile to General Stark Mountain, and 0.1 mile to a spur that leads to Glen Ellen Lodge. To the right, the LT cruises south in a mellow stroll at the beginning of a 1.8-mile jaunt to Mount Ellen's manicured peak. Dipping through a saddle and topping an intermediate knoll, the path offers a disturbing look at a strip of skiable terrain that drops off the mountain ahead. You won't be the first to wonder how the trail gets up to that peak, but in time the hindsight of a summit view will shed light on this perplexing route that sneaks along connected ridges, demanding several routine scrambles but never an inordinate climb.

Just 0.4 mile from the peak, the trail enters a 54-mile stretch of Green Mountain National Forest, where completion of a single curl convinces hikers the summit is close at hand. The tricky footing of a bouldery path leads onto an open slope with glorious western views before the trail struggles past a wooden fence that keeps skiers on the hill. Beyond the nearby Bristol Cliffs, magnificent Adirondack peaks (Mount Marcy, Mount Grant, and Whiteface) instantly grab your attention as you step onto the ski-run swath. Remember to note this unmarked entrance for the time of your return. Turning uphill, both the ski run and a trail to the left lead to a chairlift station just 100 yards below the actual summit, which is wooded and has no view.

Believe it or not, it's the ski runs that unleash phenomenal vistas and give this hike its zest. Perched atop the infamous Black Diamond Run, hikers scan the Stark Mountain ridge as it underscores Camel's Hump, Mount Mansfield, and the Worcester Range as they sweep the Green Mountains north. With Lake Champlain in the distance and buttercups at your feet, the open swaths of these grassy slopes are a great place to wander, lounge about in the sun, and consider how long you can afford to be lazy before starting your return.

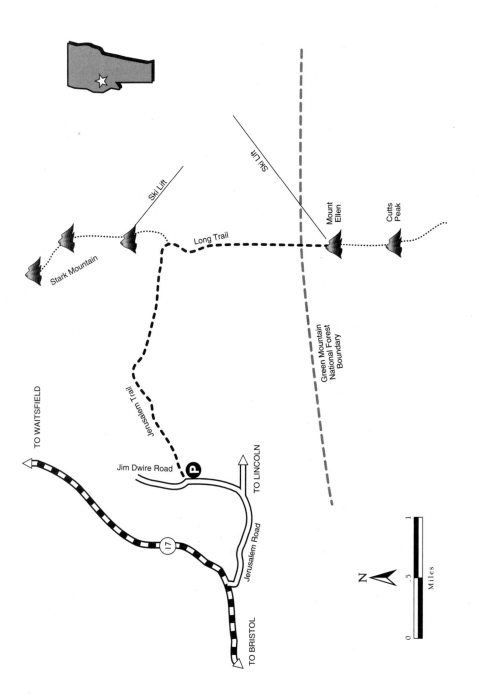

43 CAMEL'S HUMP, FORESTRY, DEAN, AND LONG TRAILS LOOP

General description:	A long, scenic day hike to Vermont's highest pristine peak and a National Natural Landmark.
General location:	Between Burlington and Montpelier, south of Interstate 89.
Length:	7.4 miles.
Difficulty:	Difficult.
Elevation gain:	2,600 feet.
Special attractions:	Summit views, rare alpine vegetation, and secluded mountain ponds.
Maps:	USGS Waterbury and Huntington quads.
For more information:	Department of Forests, Parks and Recreation, District III, 111 West Street, Essex Junction, VT 05452; (802) 879-6565.

Finding the trailhead: From Exit 10 off Interstate 89, turn south on Vermont Highway 100 and immediately turn left (east) at the junction of VT 100 and U.S. Highway 2. Follow VT 100 south and US 2 east past Winooski Street until the highways diverge 1.1 mile later. Turn right onto VT 100 South, then right again onto Main Street (the next right turn) in only 0.2 mile. Continue straight at a sharp curve after 0.3 mile entering onto River Road near Duxbury Elementary School. Follow this intermittent gravel and paved road 4.9 miles and turn left onto Camel's Hump Road. (Note: As of this writing, a shorter route to River Road via Winooski Street is interrupted by a bridge closing.)

Camel's Hump Road bears left over a bridge at 1.1 mile, continues straight over another bridge at 2.2 miles, and bears right at a fork in 3.4 miles. The road passes a parking area on the right at 3.7 miles before ending at the trailhead where additional parking is available beyond the Couching Lion Farm ranger cabin.

The hike: Backcountry ponds, improbable peaks, ridgeline scrambles, gusty vistas, and gardens of alpine beauty are among the wealth of charms displayed on the Camel's Hump loop. But, for many, it's what this mountain lacks that makes this circuit the best hike in the state. Unlike many peaks, Camel's Hump has no ski lift, inn, or auto road to mar its pristine summit, an awe-inspiring mountain environment preserved as nature intended in the 23,010-acre Camel's Hump State Park.

Unique as the profile of Camel's Hump may be, resemblance to a dromedary seems like a bit of a stretch—more like a breaking wave, I think, or a truncated dorsal fin reminiscent of those prehistoric times when the waters of Lake Vermont lapped at the base of nearby hills. In fact, the blunt stone end of the southern cliff that creates the distinctive look results from more

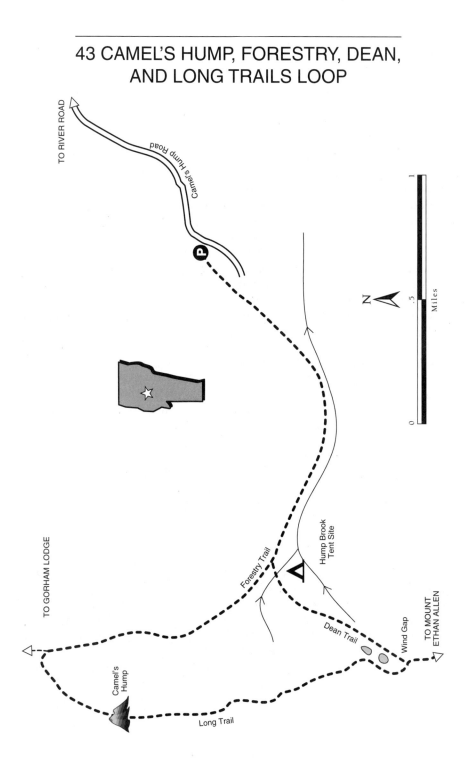

ancient forces, a typical effect of grinding glaciers that once overrode all Green Mountain summits from the north. The Forestry, Dean and Long trails loop includes a frontal approach to the vertical face of this daunting peak. It's easier than it looks, with views you won't forget.

Passing a trail sign and spring near the end of the parking lot, the well-worn Forestry Trail rises southwest at a steady pace sheltered by a canopy of hardwoods, softened by a carpet of ferns. The effort slackens after approximately 0.3 mile as the trail drifts cautiously left, avoiding a direct engagement with the slope. The path shrinks a bit, ascends through a birch and beech forest, and meets the eastern end of the Dean Trail at a major junction 1.3 miles from the trailhead. Although reason suggests that shorter routes are generally more difficult, the Forestry Trail confounds logic by branching right and maintaining a moderate pace while saving 0.6 mile. Unless you need to avoid stress, though, save it for your return. Bear left instead on a path that exacts a heavy toll in exchange for great entertainment on a scenic 2.7-mile summit loop.

The Dean Trail begins gently enough, a nearly level 0.25-mile walk that descends to cross a footbridge spanning a splendid brook, and continues easily until a spur to the Hump Brook tent site enters on the left. Ascending away from this junction, a now bony trail progresses to the top of a minor ridge and rolls to a beaver pond with the unmistakable face of Camel's Hump reflected in its pool. A large boulder at water's edge makes a marvelous spot to enjoy a snack in glorious surroundings before pushing on to other ponds huddled below imposing cliffs. The 1-mile Dean Trail concludes in Wind Gap, a rugged col between Mount Ethan Allen and Camel's Hump, where hikers turn right (north) on the Long Trail (LT), 1.7 miles from the summit.

The real fun begins in Wind Gap, as the trail gains more than 1,200 feet, rising from a spruce-fir forest to a windswept alpine peak. More quickly than you expect, the LT contorts to the top of the cliffs overlooking the familiar ponds and pops out onto an overlook with an effort only a little in excess of moderate. Now atop the southern end of a long ridge extending south from Camel's Hump, a stunning walk among blueberries and weathered evergreens treats hikers to superb northeastern views before the path briefly retreats into woods of gnarled birch. Continually bearing north, testing scrambles carry the route over intermittent boulders as the trail bobs on and off open knolls with increasingly distant views. A steady decline eventually leads to a low point on the ridge, where the trail hops up a sharp rock face and edges west under glimpses of the looming peak.

The final ascent begins with an arduous 0.33-mile climb caught between the beckoning summit and occasional Green Mountain views. Directly below the towering spire, the Alpine Trail diverges right to circumvent the top, while the LT forges on for the last 0.2 mile, a majestic rock-hopping scamper through a fragile alpine zone surrounded by sweeping vistas of lesser mountain peaks.

A mountain pond near Wind Gap reflects the summit of Camel's Hump.

Knowledgeable hikers confront an unusual problem while on this remarkable summit. Superb views of much of Vermont, the sheen of Lake Champlain, Adirondack peaks, White Mountains, and even a Canadian summit are tantalizing distractions from less-obvious delights that make Camel's Hump truly special. Imagine yourself standing on the tundra of Labrador and you'll begin to understand. Surviving all around you in a harsh alpine climate are rare and endangered arctic plants usually found 1,000 miles farther north. Cherish the rare beauty of this delicate vegetation but be certain to stay on the trail. Arctic plants tolerate brutal weather but not the tread of hikers' feet.

When it's time to depart, follow the LT down the northerly face of the mountain to a junction in a large clearing 0.3 mile from the top. Bear right (east) on the Forestry Trail for the 3.1-mile hike that moderates gradually on its straightforward descent back to the parking lot.

44   MOUNT ABRAHAM, BATTELL TRAIL

General description:	A vigorous hike up the western flank of Vermont's lowest 4,000-foot peak.
General location:	About 14 miles northeast of Middlebury, in the town of Lincoln.
Length:	5.8 miles round-trip.
Difficulty:	Intermediate.
Elevation gain:	2,500 feet.
Special attractions:	Alpine vegetation, an overnight shelter, and three-state mountain views.
Maps:	USGS Lincoln quad.
For more information:	Middlebury Ranger District, Route 7, RR 4, Box 1260, Middlebury, VT 05753; (802) 388-4362.

Finding the trailhead: In the center of Lincoln Village, turn north onto unmarked Quaker Street at a stone marker and directory sign adjacent to the Lincoln General Store. After 0.6 mile, turn right (east) onto Forest Road 350 at a second sign for the Battell Trail, and stay on this gravel road ignoring turns that branch right and left. After 2.1 miles, FR 350 narrows to one lane and leads to a parking space across the road from the trailhead.

The hike: A western approach to Mount Abraham, Vermont's fifth highest peak, the Battell Trail intercepts a portion of the Monroe Skyline near tent sites and a log shelter on the slopes of Lincoln Mountain. Aside from rare plants and fabulous views, two sugarbushes are found on this rout—the resort valley northeast of the peak and the stand of maples near the trailhead.

Tin-roofed buckets, snow-splotched woods, a horse-drawn sledge skidding from tap to tap meant sugaring in the good old days, images of another era. As the Battell Trail passes a registration box, eases through hardwoods atop a knoll, and climbs a moderate hill to a set of wooden stairs, the sugarbush that greets hikers today is strictly modern high-tech. Green plastic tubes zap through the woods like a grid of emerald lasers, but hikers and contemporary sugaring methods easily coexist. Sap lines cross well above your head as the trail modulates up a terraced slope and melds into the uniform pitch of a sidehill traverse as it exits the sugarbush.

Climbing muscles catch a break along the face of a shallow ridge before the path climbs briefly, then flattens again to span a brook on wooden planks. Just beyond this crossing, the trail directly assaults the western flank of Lincoln Mountain, the elongated parent of Mount Abraham, Mount Ellen, and other lesser peaks. With views flickering through the treetops, the route executes a 0.5-mile zigzag up a sharply angled slope then slants southeast, turning away from the summit toward a col that holds the shelter. A brisk 0.4-mile climb completes the final leg of the Battell Trail that meets a curve in the Long Trail (LT), 0.1 mile south of the campsite and 0.9 mile south of the peak.

From the Battell junction, the white-blazed LT descends 1.7 miles right (south) to Lincoln Gap. Straight ahead, a broad path rises comfortably to tent platforms and an Adirondack-style lean-to set in a glade accompanied by the sound of a gurgling brook. Even if you're not spending the night, the Battell Shelter is a logical place to stop, take a break, regain your bearings, and enjoy a refreshing snack.

North of the campsite, the LT rolls easily upward on a stony path through crowding evergreens and scrambles over exposed bedrock to disclose emerging views. Don't let the vistas overcome caution on these slippery faces of stone that carry the trail higher with the aid of sporadic footholes chipped into solid rock. Short, steep scrambles lead into the alpine zone amid reminders to stay on the trail. The path rises through krummholz, clambers over boulders, and surfaces atop a peak that greets hikers with a circle of stones and a rare collection of alpine flowers.

Scanning the horizon for points of reference, hikers find that the narrow confines of central Vermont are brought into startling focus. In the foreground to the west, Lake Champlain and the Champlain Lowlands hold back the Adirondacks that gather in New York. To the east, the Connecticut

44 MOUNT ABRAHAM, BATTELL TRAIL

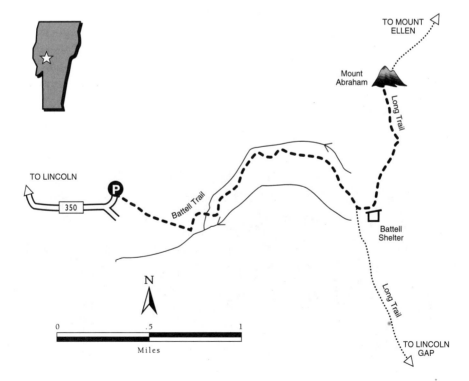

Valley forms an inner moat, protecting the Green Mountain's slender core from intruding New Hampshire peaks. To the north, angling past Mad River and the ski lifts of Sugarbush Valley, Lincoln Peak, Nancy Hanks Peak, Cutts Peak, and the taller Mount Ellen complete the contours of Lincoln Mountain in the shadow of Camel's Hump. On a southern tack, Mount Grant emerges on the far side of Lincoln Gap, the first link in a chain of peaks that crown the Breadloaf Wilderness.

THE WORCESTER RANGE

OVERVIEW

A stone's throw from Montpelier, this compact string of moderate summits stakes a claim to the best location in the state. Running north to south on a tilted axis for approximately 15 miles, the little-known peaks of the Worcester Range provide the perfect platform for superior mountain views as they parallel the central Green Mountain ridge, which erupts in massive splendor on the far side of Stowe Valley.

Among the varied perspectives found on these premier peaks, Mount Hunger clearly outshines the rest. Its extraordinary panoramas from a bold summit highlight startling visions of Mount Mansfield and Camel's Hump.

Camel's Hump and Stowe Valley from Mount Hunger's spectacular peak.

144

Though all of the peaks in the Worcester Range boast sensational mountain views, each remains unique. While exploring this glorious region, try Stowe Pinnacle for classic vistas and less climbing stress, Mount Worcester for serene hiking and a white-streaked open top, or Mount Elmore for family outings and the amusement of Balanced Rock.

45   MOUNT HUNGER, WATERBURY TRAIL

General description:	A vigorous half-day hike to the premier summit of the Worcester Range.
General location:	About 12 miles northwest of Montpelier.
Length:	3.8 miles round-trip.
Difficulty:	Intermediate.
Elevation gain:	2,300 feet.
Special attractions:	The best views of the northern Green Mountains.
Maps:	USGS Stowe quad.
For more information:	Department of Forests, Parks and Recreation, District IV, 324 North Main Street, Barre, VT 05641; (802) 479-3241.

Finding the trailhead: From Exit 10 on Interstate 89, turn north onto Vermont Highway 100, pass Ben & Jerry's (if you can), and turn right (east) onto Howard Avenue after 2.7 miles. As you drive through Waterbury Center, turn left at the second stop sign onto Maple Street, and right again in 0.2 mile onto Loomis Hill Rd. Stay on Loomis Hill Road for 1.9 miles to the junction with Sweet and Ripley roads. Turn left (north) onto Sweet Road and look very carefully for the entrance to the parking area in 1.45 miles. The driveway is a little beyond the end of the paved portion of the road and just past the entrance to a gravel opening in the woods to the right. The sign is on the right partially obscured by shrubs.

The hike: Little known to hikers outside of Vermont, Mount Hunger boasts the most picturesque summit in the range of mountains with the best location in the state. Part of the isolated Worcester chain that parallels stylish Stowe Valley and more famous peaks to the west, Mount Hunger's wind-swept crown unveils an intimate portrait of the Green Mountain's northern core. From Abraham to Ellen to Camel's Hump, from Mansfield to White-face Mountain, the crenellated mass of Vermont's highest peaks stand in stark relief just across a glacial valley. Remember this summit for sensational views.

The adventure begins on a gravelly trail that weaves beyond the parking lot through woods of dense new growth then bears right on a rootbound path after only 100 yards. Hardwood trees mature slowly as the trail loops

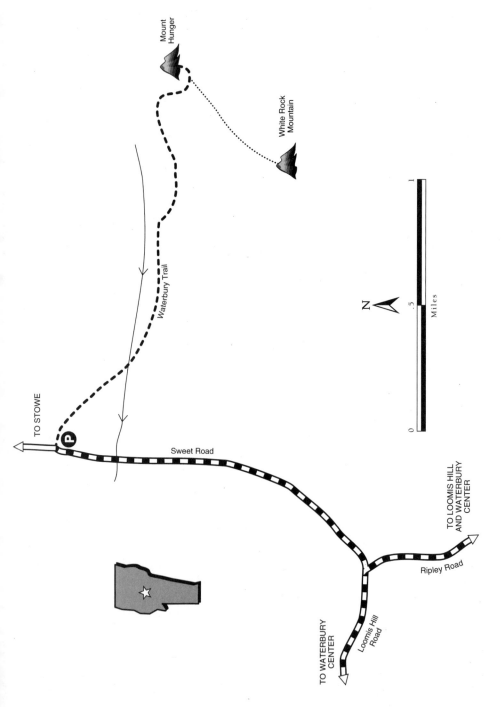

Mount Hunger

White Rock Mountain

Waterbury Trail

TO STOWE

Sweet Road

N

.5

Miles

1

0

TO LOOMIS HILL AND WATERBURY CENTER

Ripley Road

TO WATERBURY CENTER

Loomis Hill Road

up a boulder-filled slope and slants east against the grain of the hill. Aside from occasional dips and traverses that interrupt the steady pace, progress along this amiable route is best gauged by keeping track of streambed crossings. At the end of an uphill pull about halfway to the peak, a rock-clogged chasm marks the first encounter. In a normal year, splashing waters and crystal pools refresh both body and spirit in this idyllic resting spot. In dry seasons, a tumble of sizable boulders looks stranded in a meager stream.

A single long switchback leads to the second span of a brook 0.3 mile farther up the slope where a small flow channeled by rocks angles across the path. Soon, the trail bends left and levels to give hikers a break before peeled logs span the final trough, a gap that's often just a dry bed 0.4 mile from the top.

Now steeper and sporting more boulders, the end of the route stiffens once again, adding several handhold scrambles, including a few with moderate detours as an aid to hikers less daring. A short 0.2 mile from the summit, the White Rock Trail diverges right to a southerly peak less than 1 mile away, as the Waterbury Trail clambers straight ahead to pop above treeline on the exposed bedrock of Mount Hunger's summit cone.

Large ragged boulders, full 360-degree views, and bushels of blueberries tucked between random ledges outfit a summit made for exploration. More than one lap around this generous top is needed to quench a thirst for its panoramas. To the immediate north, Mount Worcester and Hogback Mountain complete the Worcester Range, leaving Jay Peak and its several neighbors still plainly in sight. To the east, scattered heights in the Northeast Kingdom stand above rolling forests while the White Mountains rise as a backdrop 60 miles distant across two states. Still, the major attraction is the Green Mountain spine that dominates the south and west, a closeup view of Vermont's highest peaks that proudly holds your gaze.

In the excitement of finding tremendous views and an expansive open summit, remember to take mental note of how you got to this top. Several unmarked trails lead off in various directions. To retrace your steps, aim between Camel's Hump and the Waterbury Reservoir when taking your leave of this memorable peak.

General description:	A recreational climb to a scenic peak overlooking the Stowe Valley.
General location:	Northwest of Montpelier, just east of Stowe village.
Length:	2.8 miles round-trip.
Difficulty:	Moderate.
Elevation gain:	1,500 feet.
Special attractions:	Green Mountain and Stowe Valley views.
Maps:	USGS Stowe quad.
For more information:	Agency of Natural Resources, Department of Forests, Parks and Recreation, District IV, 324 North Main Street, Barre, VT 05641; (802) 479-3241.

Finding the trailhead: Follow Vermont Highway 100 to the village of Stowe and turn east onto School Street in the central shopping district. After 0.3 mile, bear right at a fork onto Stowe Hollow Road, and continue straight onto Upper Hollow Road at a junction about 2 miles from the center of town. After 0.5 mile the pavement ends at the intersection with Pinnacle Road. Drive straight through the intersection to the "Pinnacle Parking Lot" 0.1 mile on the left.

The hike: Nearly 800 feet lower than Mount Hunger (see Hike 45), Stowe Pinnacle still commands breathtaking mountain views. Though the looming summits of the Worcester Range block the eastern horizon, Stowe Pinnacle's granite knobs share its neighbor's perspective on Mount Mansfield and the northern Green Mountains that tower majestically above Smugglers Notch and Stowe Valley to the west. The comparative reduction in elevation gain and easy access from the heart of Stowe village make the Pinnacle Trail the route of choice for casual recreation.

From the edge of the parking lot, a well-trod path enters a tangled field of goldenrod and apple trees as the bumpy profile of Stowe Pinnacle focuses your attention on the goal ahead. Rubbing past berry bushes at the east end of an overgrown pasture, the trail wends through sporadic cover in another former field now largely returned to woods. After bearing southeasterly over damp ground and random planks for approximately 0.2 mile, the path penetrates deeper forest, gradually increases its pitch, and crosses the bed of a stream that may be dry in the summer months.

Wobbling left and right to maintain a moderate angle against the grain of the slope, the second leg of the hike climbs steadily past mature hardwoods that bathe the path in color every fall. The trail progressively steepens as you climb, pauses for just a moment, then scrambles up a rootbound pitch to a sharp northwestern ridge. Hikers find a quick preview of summit views on a spur trail to the left before the route levels to split a tiny col, it curls south to round the peak, and descends unexpectedly before resuming its upward trek.

46 STOWE PINNACLE

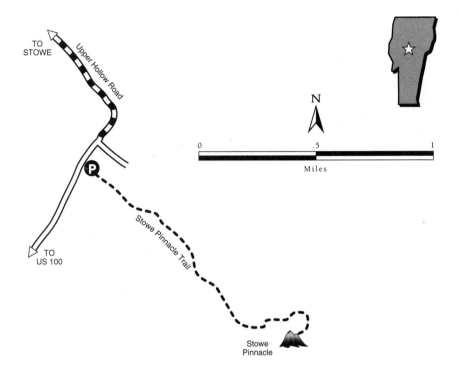

Bumping up the summit in typical mountain trail fashion, the last leg of the hike meets a sign high on a tree 0.2 mile from the top, directing the Skyline Trail left (south) toward Mount Hunger, and the Pinnacle Trail right toward the final climb of the scenic peak. The barren boulders of this modest summit lack the grandeur of its southern neighbor, but across the valley the profile of Mansfield's face remains as enticing as ever. The Worcester Range arrayed at your back inspires plans for another day.

47 MOUNT WORCESTER

General description:	A half-day hike on a lightly used trail to a summit in the Worcester Range.
General location:	About 12 miles north of Montpelier.
Length:	4.8 miles round-trip.
Difficulty:	Intermediate.
Elevation gain:	2,000 feet.
Special attractions:	Serene hiking and mountain views.
Maps:	USGS Mount Worcester quad.
For more information:	Department of Forests, Parks and Recreation, District IV, 324 North Main Street, Barre, VT 05641; (802) 479-3241.

Finding the trailhead: Travel north from Montpelier on Vermont Highway 12 and turn left (west) onto Minister Brook Road 0.15 mile past the general store and post office in Worcester village (about 80 yards past the Town Hall). Turn right onto Hampshire Hill Road after 1.5 miles and bear left in another 2.2 miles as Hancock Brook Road enters at an angle from the right. Cross a large culvert and turn left into a dirt road 0.1 mile beyond the junction. Bear right at the first fork where an arrow sign points toward the trail, and follow the lane 0.2 mile to the trailhead on the left.

The hike: After Stowe Pinnacle, Mount Hunger, or Ellmore Mountain, what does Mount Worcester offer? A hike that's quite distinct. Far removed from

Mountain views of the Worcester Range.

47 MOUNT WORCESTER

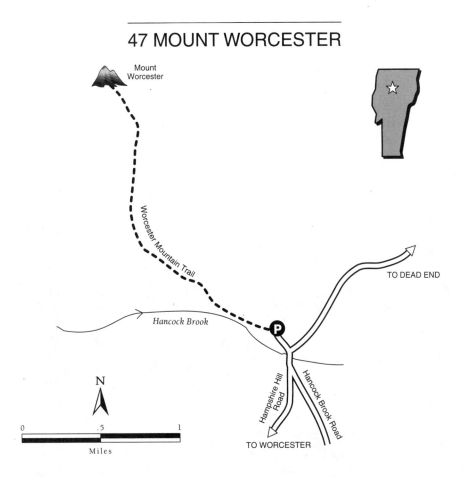

Mount
Worcester

Worcester Mountain Trail

TO DEAD END

Hancock Brook

P

Hampshire Hill Road

Hancock Brook Road

TO WORCESTER

N

0   .5   1

Miles

Stowe Valley and the gaggle of tourists west of the Worcester Range, this graceful hike emerges from a tranquil hollow that exerts its calming influence on the character of the hike. Solitary steps, peaceful streams, and a deep serenity accompany hikers to the top of this peak, contributing a generous measure of pleasure beyond the summit views.

A narrow lane extends beyond the state forest sign at the trailhead, parting the hardwoods and branching right on the far side of a brook. Already exuding a quiet aura, the trail moves staunchly upward in the rocky wash of an old logging road and crosses a second small stream after only 0.1 mile. Aiming northwest, the grade accommodates comfortable strides as the path crosses another brook that drops away into a wooded valley and then flattens to parallel the stonewashed flow of Hancock Brook. Early portions of this route remain nearly level as the path chugs upstream, passing through a glade of ferns and brambles before returning to the autumn woods by the side of the babbling stream.

A rocky vein points to Mount Worcester's top.

After angling away from Hancock Brook, a modest grade carries the trail to a cascade crossing of a smaller stream as the route twists left and right up the slope. Not steep enough to cause perspiration, too flat to remove a sweater, the ambiguous pitch of this in-between path keeps hikers guessing as they walk in the crisp fall air. Dipping briefly to skip another stream, the trail finally climbs directly upslope and spans an elevated brook on a high hogback boulder, where tiny pools and small cascades are held in check by barren rock.

Any question about layered clothing is resolved in the next 0.6 mile. Rocky and washed out in places but with the gleam of white birch sparkling on the slopes ahead, the trail tackles the heart of the ascent. Scree, slabs, and tumbled boulders make for an interesting scramble that bisects a wide cleft between sidehill outcrops as the path rises to a realm of stunted conifers, blueberries, and rumpled rock. Inspiring views urge hikers on for the last 0.3 mile while the route scales a southeastern shoulder, tracking seams of white quartz that point to the mountaintop.

Worcester Range vistas from this bumpy summit are typically superb, in spite of the fact that views straight north are made splotchy by growing scrub. Hikers scan wild perspectives on Mount Hunger, Hogback Mountain, Stowe Pinnacle, and Camel's Hump, close at hand to the south and west. In the distance to the east, the White Mountains loom as hazy lumps, and the Northeast Kingdom ranges to the border with the texture of an unmade bed. Chances are you'll have this peak to yourself. Why not use the time to investigate moss and lichen gathered in fissures at your feet, or let your mind soar with a circling hawk spiralling beyond a cloud?

48 MOUNT ELMORE

General description:	An entertaining family hike to the northernmost peak in the Worcester Range.
General location:	Near Lake Elmore Village, about 20 miles north of Montpelier.
Length:	5.2 miles round-trip.
Difficulty:	Moderate; intermediate on the alternate trail.
Elevation gain:	1,500 feet.
Special attractions:	Campground, beach, Balanced Rock, and fine fire tower views.
Maps:	USGS Morrisville quad.
For more information:	Department of Forests, Parks and Recreation, District IV, 324 North Main Street, Barre, VT 05641; (802) 479-3241.

Finding the trailhead: Follow Vermont Highway 12 north from Montpelier or south from Morrisville to the northern end of Lake Elmore. Enter

48 MOUNT ELMORE

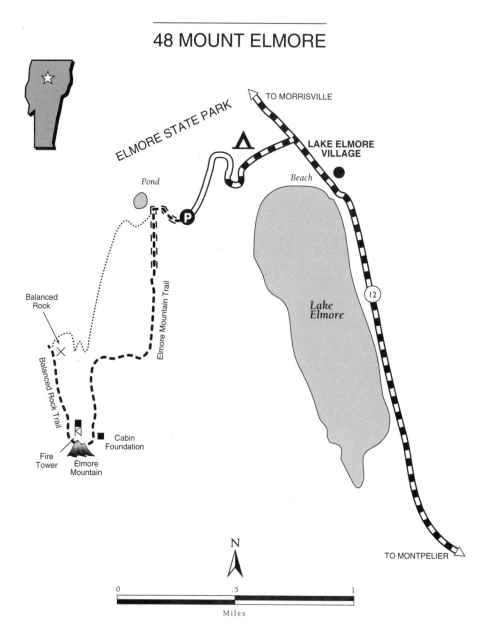

Elmore State Park on the west side of the highway, 0.4 mile north of Lake Elmore village. Stop at the contact station in season, then wind 0.8 mile uphill on the park's gravel road to a picnic shelter and metal gate across the head of the trail.

The hike: No matter how many "Balanced Rocks" are found in the world, each manages to draw a crowd. Mount Elmore's version is certainly no exception, especially since hikers can walk right up to this hulking giant and satisfy the urge to give it a shove. Even if the pivotal stone won't budge, kids of all ages enjoy this cheerful hike that starts near a beach on Elmore Lake and ends on a northern summit with great fire tower views.

Part of Elmore State Park, a popular campground at the northern end of Elmore Lake, the Elmore Mountain Trail originates near a picnic shelter at a metal gate on the main park road. Curling upward past a beaver swamp and early views of the receding lake, the gravel track ends at a picnic table where a yellow-blazed trail hops up wooden steps and continues the steady uphill trek on a wide, high-crowned path.

The pitch eases as the trail narrows into a more natural path about 0.1 mile before a 90-degree turn bends the route to the right. Rapidly ascending in short double switchbacks past mossy glacial erratics, the trail crosses a small drainage and becomes moderate again where persistent birch grow out of the top of tangled train wreck boulders. Variable blue and yellow blazes now guide the course past another overlook of the lake as the trail rounds a bulge on the mountain's flank and swiftly climbs over bedrock faces to the fieldstone chimney of a former cabin. Take a break in this small clearing that peers down on a shorefront village huddled at the northeast corner of a lake framed by checkerboard fields and mountains rolling north.

The summit tower is plainly visible from the cabin clearing, but the 0.2-mile scramble between these landmarks is extremely rocky and rough. Mud, roots, and seeping water do their best to impede your progress as hikers struggle to a T at the top of the forested peak. Fifty yards to the left, flights of tower stairs rise above treetops into prevailing winds that share the outstanding view. Camel's Hump, Mount Mansfield, Jay Peak, and the Worcester Range encircle your position while the Lamoille Valley and expansive shores of Lake Elmore soften the terrain.

Turn right at the T the Balanced Rock Trail drifts 0.5 mile north following the slow decline of the summit ridge. Weaving through spruce, fir, and mossy bogs, the path finds an outcrop with impressive Mansfield views before rambling to the top of a straight-edged boulder that reveals a northern panorama from Lake Elmore to Jay Peak. When you tear yourself away from this gorgeous outlook, Balanced Rock is perched only 200 yards farther down the slope.

Most people return the way they came. I followed an adventurous family on an alternate route that continues past Balanced Rock. Steep, muddy, and treacherous in short segments that drop off the face of the mountain, this path isn't everyone's concept of a good time as it zigzags down a ledge on the slickest mud in Vermont. If you survive the first 0.2 mile, the rest is really fun, rambling northward through a hardwood forest, turning right at another T, and returning to the gravel road just south of the beaver swamp.

THE NORTHERN UPLANDS

Northeast of Montpelier and west of Interstate 91, a rolling expanse of timbered uplands fills a widening gap between the Green Mountains and the Connecticut River. Ski slopes and alpine peaks aren't found in this rambling region, only low summits, wilderness lakes, and outstanding recreation.

The peaks and pools of Groton State Forest typify this intriguing sector. Family excursions to Owls Head or Spruce Mountain disclose landscapes of midsized mountains speckled with gleaming ponds, where wildlife and profusions of flowers stalk the wooded shores. The bumps and turns of this rumpled region hide an abundance of natural prizes. For delightful discoveries in the nooks and crannies of this out-of-the-way domain, detour to the Barr Hill Nature Preserve and reconnect with the enduring pleasures of New England ecology.

49   BARR HILL NATURE PRESERVE

General description:	A short nature walk in the northern highlands of Vermont.
General location:	Midway between Newport and Montpelier, near Caspian Lake in Greensboro.
Length:	Choice of 0.3- or 0.7-mile loops.
Difficulty:	Easy.
Elevation gain:	150 feet.
Special attractions:	Mountain profiles, diverse species of plants and wildlife, and an informative nature trail guide.
Maps:	USGS Caspian Lake; handout guides are available at the trailhead or from the address below.
For more information:	The Nature Conservancy, 27 State Street, Montpelier, Vermont 05602; (802) 229-4425.

Finding the trailhead: Follow Vermont Highway 16 to Greensboro Bend and turn northwest toward Greensboro onto Garvin Hill Road. After 2.6 miles, turn left at the stop sign near the post office then turn right half a block later at the country store. In only 0.1 mile, bear right again at a fork at the large two-story Greensboro Town Hall, proceed past the elementary school, and turn left at the next fork 0.6 mile past the Town Hall. (Look for a small green and yellow Nature Conservancy sign on a telephone pole.) In the next mile you'll pass dairy farms and a bed-and-breakfast, and enter what feels like a barnyard driveway. When you stop to open and close the

49 BARR HILL NATURE PRESERVE

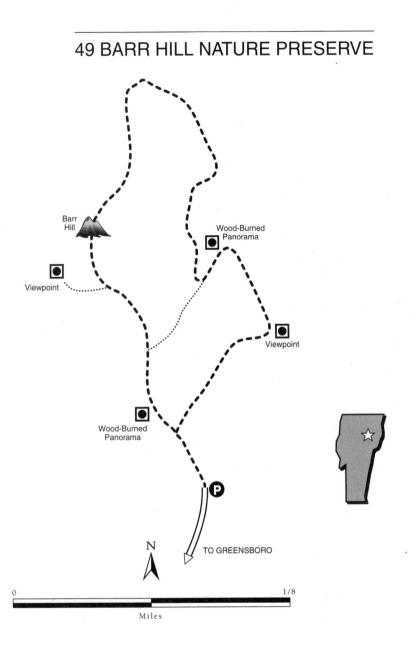

electric fence, the Barr Hill Nature Preserve sign will be standing dead ahead. Trailhead parking is still another 0.6 mile up the lane.

The hike: "Off the beaten path" acquires a whole new meaning at this 256-acre sanctuary in remote north-central Vermont. In their quest to reach the Barr Hill Nature Preserve, visitors motor along a busy barnyard lane where placid herds of Holsteins often claim the right of way. The uninitiated even learn to open and close an electric gate before arriving at a designated flat spot for parking in a field.

Hard-core types searching for rugged trail adventure should scratch Barr Hill off their list. While thrillseekers may consider this path just a loop through an overgrown pasture, hikers with a curious bent will delight in a naturalist's retreat that imparts inspiring lessons in Vermont's upland ecology. Be sure to pick up a nature trail guide from a box near the trailhead. This superb brochure makes Barr Hill's plants, animals, history, and views familiar to the newest visitor and acts as a key to lettered stations scattered along the hike.

After signing in at the registration box, follow the trail past dwarf junipers and newborn maple trees to engaging early views. A wood-burned profile of the Green Mountains from Killington to Madonna Peak mirrors horizons to the south and west before the path moves on to look at nearby Caspian Lake framed by arbor-vitae. At station D, hikers can bear right to shorten the loop and find a picnic site, or cross the rubble of an old stone wall to complete an entire circuit that you really shouldn't miss.

Diversity is the catchword for this hike, with abundant habitats and microenvironments ably explained by The Nature Conservancy's Barr Hill guide. Forest zones, ferny swales, glacial gouges, metamorphosed rock, and bird, tree, and moss identifications are topics in a walking seminar as the loop passes outcrops near the summit, enters a glade of spruce, and skims deserted fields before returning to the upper end of the shortcut path. Turn right if you're ready for a picnic and a second view of Caspian Lake. Otherwise continue a modest descent to another wood-burned panorama of mountain peaks that rise in the east/northeast and stroll through lessons in limestone erosion that complete the circular path. Barr Hill is meant to instill a sense of stewardship and commitment to the natural world. Hikers have an excellent chance of leaving this secluded place peacefully reconnected to the resources that sustain life.

50 GROTON STATE FOREST, KETTLE POND TRAIL, AND OWLS HEAD

General description:	A 3-hour hike around a forest pond and a short walk to Owls Head Mountain.
General location:	About halfway between Montpelier and Saint Johnsbury.
Length:	A 3-mile circle of Kettle Pond; 0.25 mile round-trip to the summit of Owls Head.
Difficulty:	Kettle Pond, moderate; Owls Head, easy.
Elevation gain:	Kettle Pond, negligible; Owls Head, 200 feet.
Special attractions:	Wildlife, wildflowers, and wonderful shore views; Green Mountain vistas from Owls Head.
Maps:	Trail maps are available at campgrounds in the state forest or from the address below.
For more information:	Agency of Natural Resources, Department of Forests, Parks and Recreation, District V, 184 Portland Street, St. Johnsbury, VT, 05819; (802) 748-8787.

Finding the trailhead: Vermont Highway 232 runs through the heart of Groton State Forest, forming a link between U.S. Highways 2 and 302. The parking lot for the Kettle Pond Trail is directly off the west side of VT 232. From the south, the trailhead is 7 miles north of US 302, 4.9 miles past the entrance to the forest, and just beyond the access road for the Kettle Pond group camping area. From the north, the trailhead is 1 mile south of the Owls Head auto road.

The hike: More than 25,000 acres of ponds, beaches, campgrounds, and trails within easy reach of the capitol of Vermont, make Groton State Forest a premier choice for family recreation. Of all the varied attractions in this timberland retreat, Owls Head mountain undoubtedly enjoys the most notable reputation. With the aid of a convenient auto road, campers, hikers, and casual passersby find a short trail to one of the finest views in the Green Mountain State at the top of this prominent peak. For a few discriminating visitors, though, the Kettle Pond Trail presents Owls Head in a very different light. Far removed from the pressing crowds, this private view from the shore of a wild wood pond envelops hikers in a natural realm at the heart of this preserve.

A simple counter-clockwise walk around an oblong lake, the Kettle Pond Trail uncovers nature in a multitude of forms. Leaving the north end of the parking lot on a path between random stones, the trail runs a 70-yard gauntlet of birch and evergreens before opening onto a wetland thicket thinned by local beaver. Blue blazes bend the rough-hewn trail to the right as it skirts the unkempt marsh and temporarily divides it. To the right, a short prong leads to the first of several adirondack shelters that dot the circumfer-

50 GROTON STATE FOREST, KETTLE POND TRAIL, AND OWLS HEAD

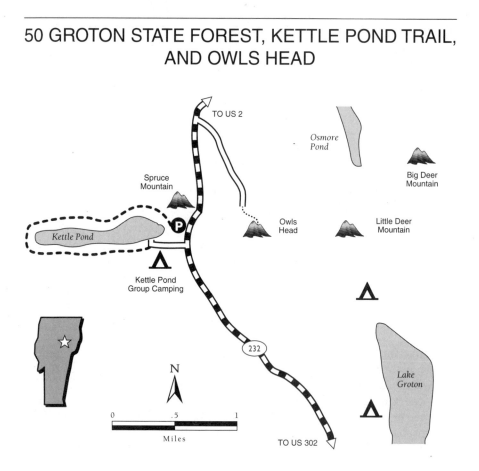

ence of the lake. To the left, the main trail leads directly to the shore and a soothing white birch glade where worn tracks open expansive views across the breadth of the pond.

Saw grass, Labrador tea, rhododendron, and assorted berries accompany an intimate walk along a lapping shore, while moose and deer prints pepper the path, an owl floats overhead, and as the call of a loon raucously echoes from the depths of a hidden cove. About one-third of the way down the length of the northern side, large boulders block the water's edge and several stones contribute to tricky footing in a wet section of trail. As the path swings left following a curve that ends the first lobe of this extended lake, the looming face of Owls Head stares back from across the pond, part of a dazzling tableau framed by evergreens that line the crooked shore.

By the time hikers reach the second lobe of the pond about halfway down the northern side, they realize that the time needed to complete this trek exceeds what the mileage on the map implies. Too many temptations slow your pace as you meander along the shore, poking about flowering plants

Kettle Pond and Camel's Hump attract families to the Owl's Head Summit.

and listening for skittish loons. Arriving eventually at a sequestered cove on the west end of the lake, the trail edges up the slope into the piney woods, passes a tilting shelter, and swings wide into the forest to keep footing as dry as possible as it rounds the tip of the pond.

Frankly, the north shore path is a lot more fun than the return trail on the south. Explore as far as you want, but don't feel the need to finish the entire loop. Fields of glacial erratics roughen the far end of the southside route, but a peaceable path soon reappears after ducking behind a cabin near the start of the eastbound trek. The return trail never strays far from the lake, but it lacks the same entertaining contact with the shore and ends at a group camping area on the east end of Kettle Pond. To find your way back, turn right on the campground driveway that intersects VT 232 about 70 yards south of the trailhead parking lot.

In spite of a crowded trail, you really shouldn't leave Groton State Forest without turning the tables on this lakeside walk. Drive 1 mile north from the trailhead and turn right onto the Owls Head auto road. Amid the magnificent vistas at the top you'll recognize Kettle Pond, a slender arm that points just to the left of distinctive Camel's Hump.

51 SPRUCE MOUNTAIN

General description:	A 3- to 4-hour family hike through a state forest to the summit of Spruce Mountain.
General location:	About 12 miles east of Montpelier, midway between U.S. Highways 2 and 302.
Length:	4.3 miles round-trip.
Difficulty:	Moderate.
Elevation gain:	1,300 feet.
Special attractions:	Peaceful woodlands with reliable fire tower views.
Maps:	USGS Knox Mountain quad.
For more information:	Agency of Natural Resources, Department of Forests, Parks and Recreation, District V, 184 Portland Street, St. Johnsbury, VT 05819; (802) 748-8787.

Finding the trailhead: From the junction of Vermont Highway 110 and U.S. Highway 302 near East Barre, continue 1.1 mile east on US 302 and turn left onto a paved road following signs to Plainfield. This road passes the City of Barre water supply and views of Spruce Mountain, before the pavement ends and hikers bear right at a fork onto East Hill Road, 5.4 miles from US 302. In the span of 0.8 mile, this gravel road tops a rise with magnificent views, dips into a hollow, and begins to climb another hill when Spruce Mountain Road enters on the right. Turn right onto this unmarked gravel road and bear left in 0.3 mile at a fork marked with signs to the "Summit Trail 1/2M." At the end, you'll find a small parking area near the

51 SPRUCE MOUNTAIN

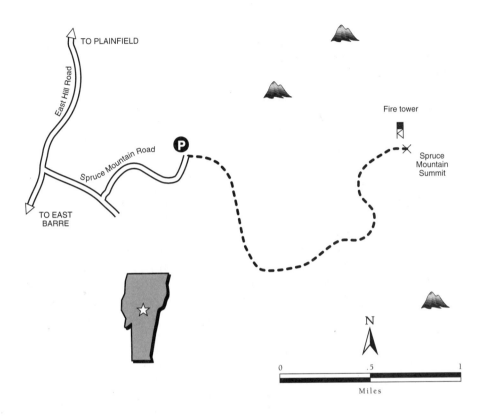

remains of the old gate and a larger space about 80 yards up the rough dirt road close to a newer trailhead.

From the north, East Hill Road can be reached from the blinker lights on US 2 in Plainfield. Turn south at the blinkers, immediately dip downhill, cross a bridge, and bear left. A very scenic 4-mile drive leads to the left turn onto Spruce Mountain Road.

The hike: Superb family hikes to remarkable views are rare in the east-central portion of the state, a rambunctious region of low summits that fill a widening gap between the Green Mountains and the Connecticut River. This route, then, holds a pleasant surprise. Aided by an old fire tower re-cycled as an observation deck, the Spruce Mountain trail rises above a thick cloak of evergreens to marvelous views that overlook Groton State Forest, the nascent Winooski River, and countless peaks that scatter to the far corners of northern New England.

From a red post that serves as the trailhead, a level jeep track curls east from the parking area far below the glint of the sun on the summit's silver tower. Dipping downhill, the path skims past gleaming birch and calmly advances toward the base of the mountain that blinks through the woods on your left. The sound of a brook whispers from the east as the track curves slowly south and climbs away from the peak. When the trail finally returns to an eastern course, the steady grade eases along a knoll with partial mountain views and enters the clearing of an old logging yard at the halfway point of the outbound hike.

Beyond the clearing, a blue blaze marks a narrower path that extends the arching route and commences a brief ascent through woods of birch and evergreens. Swinging north, the rocky trail flattens, spans a brook and several wet spots near the mountain's base, and begins the true ascent. Meandering upward past an immense glacial erratic that hunkers at the side of the trail, the forest path maintains reasonable footing, as it slabs across slick faces of ledge on the mountain's southwestern slope. Slowly, the trail curls right, weaving through ferny glades of gnarled birch and stunted hardwoods that lie just below the summit until sliding through a narrow channel of crowding conifers in the final yards to the fire tower.

At the peak, a small clearing between the tower and the foundation of an old ranger cabin forms a ready-made picnic spot with local views of Signal and Burnt mountains farther south and east. After a little refreshment, scale the shining tower, rise above the trees, and discover outstanding views that await from the windowless cabin atop the column. Camel's Hump, Mount Mansfield, Jay Peak, and the snowcapped summits of the White Mountains can all be identified from here. Less prominent Lake Groton and Peacham Pond mark Groton State Forest that spreads to the north and east (see Hike 50), while the valley of the Winooski River hides Montpelier to the west. Be cautious as you swing your gaze to all points of the compass. The open stairwell in the cabin floor makes a hazardous first step when you're ready to return.

THE NORTHERN BORDER

OVERVIEW

Hike the Long Trail north from Mount Mansfield, following the Green Mountain crest, and everyone knows you'll come to Jay Peak before touching Canada's border. What else you'll find in this 66-mile stretch, most people haven't a clue .

The bulk of this region is too remote for the usual day hiking crowd, making established paths outside of the Long Trail corridor few and far between. The trails that do exist are hardscrabble routes that fit unruly terrain, well suited to independent hiking types not afraid to go it alone. Scrambly, steep, hard to follow, and a little rough around the edges, the trails to Mount Norris and Burnt Mountain are characteristic of this untamed region with rocky knolls, barren outcrops, and marvelous north-country views.

Ritterbush Pond is the northern exception, a family hike to a nature preserve, a tiny Long Trail cabin, and mysterious Devil's Gulch.

52 BURNT MOUNTAIN

General description:	A half-day hike to a little-known peak in remote north-central Vermont.
General location:	Between Saint Albans and Newport, south of Jay Peak.
Length:	4.4 miles round-trip.
Difficulty:	Intermediate.
Elevation gain:	1,000 feet.
Special attractions:	Uncrowded trails and views of Hazen's Notch.
Maps:	USGS Hazen's Notch quad.
For more information:	Hazen's Notch Association, Montgomery Center, Vermont 05471; (802) 326-4789.

Finding the trailhead: Vermont Highway 58 runs east from Montgomery Center beginning about 80 yards south of the junction of Vermont Highways 118 and 242 in the middle of town. The pavement ends before a right turn onto Rossier Road 2.1 miles from the village. Bear right at a fork in Rossier Road about 250 yards after the turn. The High Ponds Preserve parking area is 0.3 mile farther at the end of the road.

The hike: Between Mount Mansfield and Jay Peak, the Cold Hollow Range forms the end of the Green Mountain line, 20 miles of scaled-back summits that stretch to the top of Vermont. Tucked off a gravel highway in the vicinity of Hazen's Notch, Burnt Mountain is an unsung summit just east of the Cold Hollow peaks that hikers rarely stumble across, but efforts by a local nonprofit group may eventually change all that. Part of a 10-mile network of paths maintained by the Hazen's Notch Association for nonmotorized public use, the newly blazed Burnt Mountain Trail boasts a sense of adventure and great views of the nearby notch. On a recent hike, light use and scant blazes in a timbered section put route-finding skills to the test, but new signs, more blazes, and better parking are in the works as this guidebook goes to press.

Intended as a hiking path and winter snowshoe route, the first steps on the Burnt Mountain Trail pass through a gate that bars vehicles from a forest road shaded by the summit ahead. Passing 50 yards beyond a small

52 BURNT MOUNTAIN

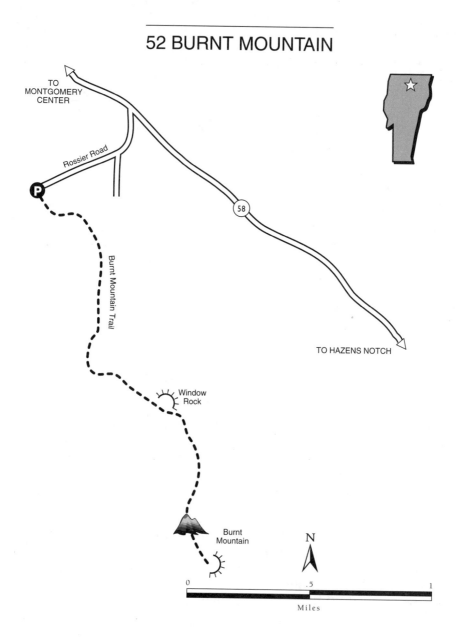

TO MONTGOMERY CENTER

Rossier Road

P

58

TO HAZENS NOTCH

Burnt Mountain Trail

Window Rock

Burnt Mountain

N

0 .5 1

Miles

beaver pond on the left, a blue-blazed trail soon turns away from the road, 2 miles from the summit and about 1 mile from the viewpoint at Window Rock. Here and there, ribbons mark a faint corridor of trampled ferns and vegetation as the path crosses a brook where a bridge is planned and wends its way through a tangle of young forest. Be alert for a sharp right turn marked by an eye-level arrow before the path ascends into a segment of woods that shows scars from recent logging. During my visit, blowdowns and missing blazes made the going tough in this limited section, but a moderate climb overcame the disturbance and found a more trustworthy path.

A stiff climb makes Window Rock seem more than 1 mile from the trailhead, but its small outcrop grants clear views of Hazen's Notch and local mountains. Consider this halfway point as a compromise destination for hikers who would like to avoid the adventurous end of the trip.

Keep a sharp eye on the ribbon blazes as you continue past Window Rock. The trail climbs crisply for about 150 yards, turns right just beyond a minor ledge, and begins a short, difficult scramble to a tiny gorge. With a bigger ledge looming on the right, the path turns left up a sheer bank then goes sharply right again after passing the uphill end of a barren rock slab. Have faith in this woodsy trail, which now gets genuinely steep as it crawls through soft forest footing directly upslope.

The pitch moderates in a birch glade near the top, where the path rolls easily toward a summit spattered with signs of moose. The route is brushy in spots and leads to a wooded peak that offers nothing in the way of views. To find your just reward, keep following the trail that drops off the east face of the summit and bears south through spruce and fir. After 0.2 mile this path sputters to a ragged end at a slender blueberry outcrop with superb views of the mountainous yawn of Hazen's Notch and the towering summit of Jay Peak catching storm clouds farther north.

53 JAY PEAK

General description:	A half-day hike to the northernmost Green Mountain peak.
General location:	About 15 miles west of Newport; 6 miles south of the Canadian border.
Length:	3.4 miles round-trip.
Difficulty:	Intermediate.
Elevation gain:	1,700 feet.
Special attractions:	A terrific circle of summit views with an international flair.
Maps:	USGS Jay Peak quad.
For more information:	None available.

Finding the trailhead: A spacious Long Trail parking lot is located on the south side of Vermont Highway 242 at the crest of the Green Mountain ridge, 6.3 miles east of Montgomery Center or 5.1 miles west of the village of Jay (1.4 miles west of the Jay Peak Ski Resort). The trailhead is across the road.

The hike: There's no mistaking Jay Peak, the most northerly Green Mountain summit, that rises in splendid isolation just 6 miles south of Canada's

53 JAY PEAK

53. JAY PEAK

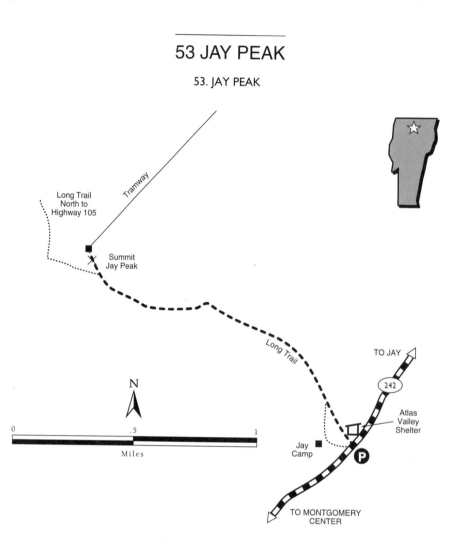

Long Trail
North to
Highway 105

Tramway

Summit
Jay Peak

Long Trail

N

0 .5 1

Miles

TO JAY

242

Atlas
Valley
Shelter

Jay
Camp

P

TO MONTGOMERY
CENTER

border. Seen from the east, Jay's angular facets of bare rock resemble a European Alp, complete with a year-round tramway station cantilevered off the top. From other directions, the mountain looks less severe, its sculptured multi-mounded appearance more inviting to a hiker's approach. Jay Peak can draw a crowd, but even after mingling with tourists assembled on the tramway deck, the climb is lots of fun with refreshing views that add a touch of international flair.

The 1.7-mile Long Trail (LT) journey begins on a narrow path that coincides briefly with the Catamount (cross-country ski) Trail as they ascend north from the highway, passing a day-use shelter still within sight of the road. Both trails pause at a set of directional signs and a hiker registration box before the Jay Loop Trail diverges 10 yards later to carry the ski path on a short descent to a spring and overnight cabin. Preliminaries over, the LT sets to its task of completing a moderate climb under cover of deciduous forest, flirting on occasion with the heavier burden of tackling a steeper slope. By the time the Jay Loop Trail rejoins the route 0.3 mile uphill, hikers have already climbed high enough to enjoy fragments of mountain vistas to the west.

With the slope rising on the right, a strong, steady climb proceeds for the better part of 0.4 mile before the angle of the hill subsides and the path relaxes. First nudging right to slant more sharply upslope then veering back left, the trail courses through the woods several yards below a ski run that plunges toward the east. Reliable footing suffers in the next 0.25 mile. Stepping over boulders, slanted slabs, and loose collections of stones, the trail curls through wind-blown evergreens, scampers over snow gun lines, and finally bursts into sunshine with unending southern views.

From the vantage of an open slope, a unique tower and a choice of routes plainly pop into view. While the ski run provides 0.2 mile of carefree walking, most hikers put smiles on their faces by following blazes across the slope, scrambling up a rocky ridge, and conquering a peak that rises only a few steps higher than the tramway door. The view from the top is a marvel. Mount Royal rises in Montreal only 60 miles to the north and west, while the glimmer of Lake Memphremagog straddles Canada's nearby border. Mount Mansfield's Nose, Camels' Hump, and Mount Washington's massive hulk complete a circle of mountain views, but the exceptional vista from this northern peak is the one directly south. Like no other summit in New

Jay Peak, Vermont's northernmost Green Mountain climb.

England, Jay Peak confirms its role as the head of a Green Mountain chain that marches over the horizon, grandly dividing sweeping valleys, retreating in parallel planes.

54   MOUNT NORRIS

General description:	A half-day hike to an uncivilized peak with tremendous north-country views.
General location:	About 17 miles southwest of Newport.
Length:	3.5 miles round-trip.
Difficulty:	Intermediate.
Elevation gain:	1,300 feet.
Special attractions:	Summit views of northern Vermont.
Maps:	USGS Albany quad.
For more information:	Camp Ranger, Mount Norris Scout Reservation, P.O. Box 28, Eden Mills, VT 05653; (802) 635-7463.

Finding the trailhead: Look for a dirt driveway on the west side of Vermont Highway 100, 3.25 miles north of the junction of VT 100 and Vermont Highway 118, 2 miles north of Eden Mills, or 0.1 mile north of the Mount Norris Scout Reservation. The driveway is the entrance to a logging yard. Be sure to park off the road without blocking the right-of-way.

The hike: Knee deep in skid road mud searching for missing blazes, I confess that a certain negativity colored my first impressions of this hike. I got over it at the top. Fact is, the wild scrambles and great views concealed on this untamed peak are worth some aggravation.

Two trails lead to the summit, but in 1995 parts of the Dean Trail were reduced to nothing but muck. The bottom end of the Mount Norris Trail also suffered in the process, but hikers with good intuition should still be able to find their way and not be bothered by mud. Conditions could also change at any time, and the Scout camp that cares for the trails has plans to upgrade the route. Take this description with a grain of salt.

Stationed at the trailhead, hikers find themselves on a dirt driveway that enters a busy logging yard with a view of Mount Norris. Follow the fork of a skid road to the right as it angles across the clearing toward a vigorous brook that nips the corner of the lot. A bright green blaze on a fir tree pulls the route north up a freshly graded road that tracks the stream to an older clearing after about 0.5 mile. Here the fun begins.

Approximately halfway up the length of the second clearing, the Mount Norris Trail bears right (northeast) as a narrow path and rapidly finds a logging road shooting directly up the slope. As the track ascends, mixed hardwoods furnish great habitat for deer, moose, and partridge. Occasional

54 MOUNT NORRIS

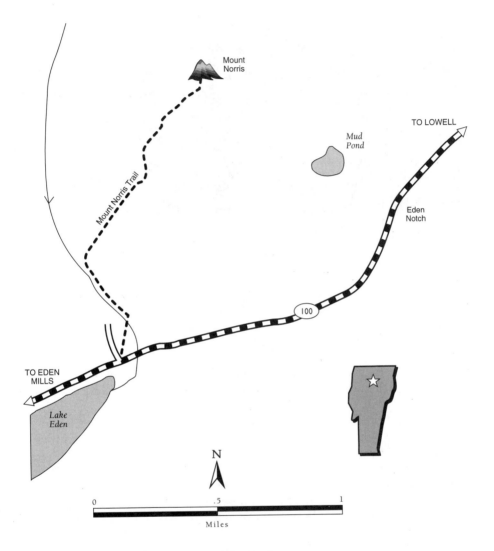

blazes come and go obscurely in the woods. During my visit, following the skid road seemed like the best bet until it turned oddly right and I spotted an orange ribbon on a smaller fork that kept going straight ahead. Lucky to find it, I guess. Hope your fortune is equally good.

Blue blazes, orange blazes, and marker ribbons become more consistent

Lake Eden and the Green Mountains reward experienced hikers on Mount Norris's untamed peak.

the higher you climb, just as the effort gets more intense. Passing to the right of a large glacial erratic at the tip of a hanging outcrop, a short spur scrambles to introductory views before the main trail splits a gap in a looming ledge and climbs at severe angles to the top of a narrow ridge. Trees reach up from both sides as the route turns left, skirts the 40-foot face of a mossy rock, and struggles to a height ahead. Wriggle up and over the rock faces of this un-named knoll then descend to a shallow col where brambles and scores of trillium underline the base of an outrageous cliff

Sixty yards of difficult handhold climbing get you to the top of this impossible pitch, where the path curlicues to stunning views from open rock. Sorry! It's not the peak. Bear left into another col for the last 0.4 mile, which constitutes less of a test as it dips, bends, clambers, and curls to your final destination. Remember, if you're in the woods, you haven't reached the top.

After all you've been through, you deserve the views, which are nothing short of superb. Looking south, Lake Eden directs your gaze to Mount Mansfield, Camel's Hump, and the heart of the Green Mountain Range. Closer at hand, Vermont Highway 100 swoops through a verdant valley, a secluded land of conifer hills that appear to be winning the struggle for any pastures that still remain.

General description:	A half-day hike to a scenic outcrop and narrow chasm with an overnight option at Ritterbush Camp.
General location:	About 22 miles southwest of Newport.
Length:	5 miles round-trip.
Difficulty:	Moderate.
Elevation gain:	500 feet.
Special attractions:	Babcock Preserve, Ritterbush Lookout, and magical Devil's Gulch.
Maps:	USGS Hazens Notch and Eden quads.
For more information:	For the Babcock Preserve only—The Nature Conservancy, 27 State Street, Montpelier, VT 05602; (802) 229-4425.

Finding the trailhead: From the junction of Vermont Highways 118 and 109 in Belvedere Corners, drive south on VT 118 2 miles to the Long Trail (LT) crossing. Park well off the road near a sign for the LT south.

The hike: Looking for a Long Trail (LT) adventure without a big mountain climb? This mellow hike to a backcountry pond and intimate magical chasm may be just what you had in mind. Day trippers can easily accomplish this hike on a summer afternoon, but a primitive camp at the edge of the trail provides another dimension. Only backpackers are able to tour peculiar

Basic Long Trail shelter at intriguing Ritterbush Camp.

White blazes mark the Long Trail through magical Devil's Gulch.

Devil's Gulch when the misty gloam of dawn or dusk heightens its eerie spell.

One of my favorite low-key hikes, the route to Ritterbush Pond follows the LT south on a comfortable ramble beginning at the height of a rolling ridge. Ascents are slow and gradual on the relaxed contours of this amiable crest as the trail ducks under a small powerline, enters a depression in the

55 RITTERBUSH POND AND DEVIL'S GULCH

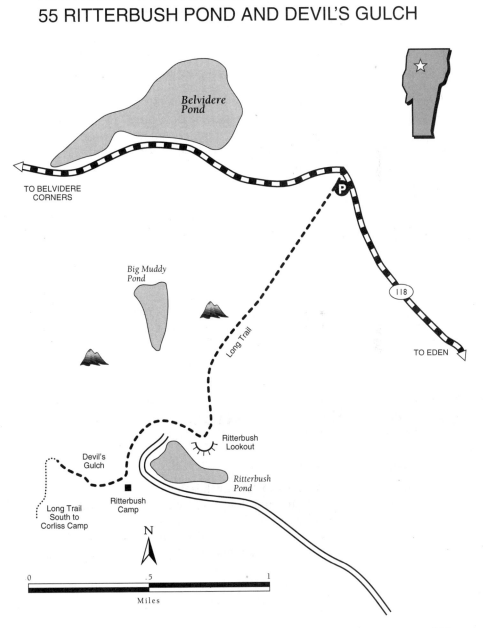

broadened ridge, and bounces west to the top of a gentle slope. A long, steady cruise whisks by blackberry bushes as the trail reaches its highest point with little fanfare and modest effort.

Skimming past a forest wetland, the trail glides south just above a shallow drainage as pools of afternoon sunlight gleam in the woods ahead. Such pools hold promise, of course. In this case, a winding descent that leads to Ritterbush Lookout, a picturesque outcrop 200 feet above the quiet waters of Ritterbush Pond. More than a thousand acres surrounding this backcountry lake form the Babcock Nature Preserve, a rugged realm managed for educational purposes, rich with birds and wildlife.

Leaving the lookout on the right, stone steps drop the trail precipitously down the slope. The path then skirts high above the shore to gain the western end of the pond. About 70 yards beyond a mossy brook, a side path runs 0.2 mile left to a woods road that allows exploration of the lakefront and an active beaver lodge. For now, though, roll with the LT up and down the slant of a hill, cross another brook, and stumble 200 yards up a ledge to tiny Ritterbush Camp. A basic accommodation perched on a scoured rock, this cozy cabin entertains hikers with distant views of Ritterbush Pond glowing faintly in the evening light.

The LT literally touches the corner of Ritterbush Camp, just 0.2 mile from the conclusion of the hike in the dank, cloistered confines of astounding Devil's Gulch. Up to 70 feet high and less than 25 yards across, the walls of this stone-clad cleft are smothered by gnarled trees that clutch at head-high boulders along the path. Water seeps and trickles through fissures still unseen, ferns and moss add layers of green to human-sized shards of rock, and hikers sneak beneath a tepee of ancient fallen stone. Little light penetrates this marvelous crevasse where canopies of leaves arch high above the trail and fallen trees hang in space bridging the narrow top. Stay for the foggy twilight and you're sure to understand why a fiendish name perfectly suits this singular abyss.

THE NORTHEAST KINGDOM

OVERVIEW

Comprising three counties in far northeastern Vermont, the Northeast Kingdom generally brings to mind long, cold winters, hardscrabble farms, and miles of evergreen forest. But life here is more complex. Independent lifestyles, prosperous dairies, and prolific displays of nature confound the conventional wisdom in a region that includes both lakeside cliffs and lumpy fields melding into Quebec.

Like its varied terrain, hikes in the Northeast Kingdom demonstrate an extensive repertoire. Climb a tower to incredible views, perch on a towering cliff, or guide the family to a scrambling peak over breathtaking faces of rock. Of course, fishing holes and miles of forest also receive their due, together with flowers in a delicate bog most hikers will find unique.

56   BURKE MOUNTAIN

General description:	A drive-up summit with a network of trails to an observation tower and secondary peak.
General location:	About 12 miles north of Saint Johnsbury.
Length:	Round-trips of 0.2 to 1.4 miles, depending on choice of options.
Difficulty:	Moderate, with easy access to the summit tower.
Elevation gain:	100 to 300 feet.
Special attractions:	Mountaintop walks and great views.
Maps:	USGS Burke Mountain quad.
For more information:	Department of Forests, Parks and Recreation, District V, 184 Portland Street, St. Johnsbury, VT 05819; (802) 748-8787.

Finding the trailhead: From Exit 23 off Interstate 91, drive 2.1 miles north on U.S. Highway 5 and bear right onto Vermont Highway 114. Pass the post office in East Burke and turn right onto a paved road, following signs for the Burke Mountain Resort. The toll road to the top of the mountain forks left after 2.2 miles. The toll road is open from late May to mid-October between 9 a.m. and 6 p.m.

The hike: A solitary peak in the Northeast Kingdom's southern tier, Burke Mountain is a special case. While a ramshackle trail runs from bottom to top, it also converges with an auto road that leads to a summit tower. Is it better to hike or drive? Depends on your point of view. Overgrown vistas, a confusing route, and a 0.75-mile walk on a newly graded access road persuaded me that climbing the full height of this mountain wasn't the best idea. Most hikers will be happy to pay $3 per car, drive to the top, and cobble together a network of paths that link the mountain's highlights in a delightful summit tour.

First priority is the tower. Hikers are now prohibited from walking a few yards up another driveway and curling past a transmission station to reach their destination. Choose instead the Profile Trail, which departs from the far end of the parking lot diagonally opposite the ski lift at the end of the auto road. Bear left about 20 yards into the woods, then spin right 40 yards later following blue/white blazes in the direction of the tower.

In the course of 0.4 mile, the white trail descends through evergreen woods, where a blue trail diverges to the left, and skims below rocky ledges on a pleasant walk that's much more inviting than the typical path found on

56 BURKE MOUNTAIN

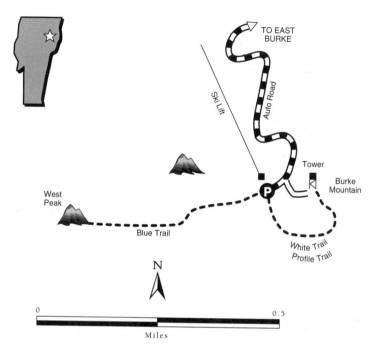

drive-up peaks. Rising through the middle of a mossy, miniature chasm beneath a boulder overhang where no one should bump his or her head, this scenic roundabout path promptly passes the upper end of the blue trail shortcut and finds the base of the summit tower after only a moderate climb. To complete your effort, scramble to the top of the tower, where tremendous 360-degree views reveal Quebec and White Mountain ranges soaring in closer proximity than Vermont's own Green Mountain peaks.

West Peak is the next destination. Back at the far end of the parking lot, the broad swath of a ski trail opens a northwest view of Mount Pisgah and Mount Hor (see Hikes 57 and 58) as it sweeps past the wooded knoll of West Peak on the left. Follow an older section of blue-blazed trail that enters the woods to the south (left) of the ski run and pass weather-beaten signs on your way 0.3 mile downhill. Several homemade paths veer off to picnic spots in the ski slope grass before the trail meets a five-way junction about 80 yards below West Peak. Both uphill paths have a log shelter at the top, but the blue trail curls to a stop on barren boulders with outstanding Presidential Range views before making its way past the shelter to a good vista looking south.

If these gentle explorations aren't good enough, hard-core hikers can find the bottom of the West Peak Trail (Red Trail) by turning into the Sherburne

Beacons of the Northeast Kingdom, Mount Pisgah and Mount Hor as seen from Burke Mountain.

Base Lodge, 1.2 miles off Vermont Highway 114. Start walking on the dirt road that leaves the far end of the lower parking lot and reaches a red gate after 100 yards. On my last trip, extensive regrading of the road suddenly ended 0.1 mile before a red-blazed trail turned left into the woods just beyond a tiny culvert at a small sign at the height of land. It's a stiff climb. After 0.8 mile follow a woods road left for 50 yards then turn right past another log shelter. Beyond the lean-to, a blue-blazed trail leads you to West Peak.

---

57 MOUNT PISGAH

General description:	A 3-hour hike to breathtaking cliffs overlooking Lake Willoughby.
General location:	East of Interstate 91 between Saint Johnsbury and Derby Line.
Length:	4 miles round-trip.
Difficulty:	Moderate.
Elevation gain:	1,600 feet.
Special attractions:	Spectacular clifftop views and possible chances for sighting hawks and falcons.
Maps:	USGS Sutton quad.
For more information:	Department of Forests, Parks and Recreation, District V, 184 Portland Street, St. Johnsbury, VT 05819; (802) 748-8787.

See Map on Page 185

Finding the trailhead: From Interstate 91, Exit 23, follow U.S. Highway 5 north 9.4 miles to the village of West Burke. Bear right at the general store onto Vermont Highway 5A and proceed 5.6 miles to a parking lot on the left (west) side of the road shortly before the highway descends to the lake. A Willoughby State Forest trailhead sign is directly across the road.

The hike: Chiseled cliffs plunging to opposing shores of a blue water northern lake endow Mounts Pisgah and Hor with unrivalled landmark status. Beacons of the Northeast Kingdom, the bulging profiles of these twin mounds carved by glacial action guide vacationers to the 5-mile gouge known as Lake Willoughby. Boating, fishing, swimming, and camping thrive on this popular lake, and visitors with an interest in hiking can climb to an overlook from both peaks. A moderate family trek, the stirring hike on the Mount Pisgah Trail on Lake Willoughby's eastern shore climbs to rocky aeries high on precipitous cliffs with views of faraway mountains and white caps on the lake.

The hike begins with variety you don't expect. After a sign greets hikers 20 feet down the embankment from the road, the south end of the Mount

Lake Willoughby points north from the Pisgah cliffs.

Pisgah Trail extends 100 yards northwest to cross the middle of a large beaver pond on two sections of a wooden bridge. Topping a ridge on the opposite bank, the path curls left, skimming ever higher to the far end of the pond where ridge melds into hillside and the trail bears right to angle upslope. Less than 0.25 mile from the pond, the trail abruptly turns back to the left, briskly climbing past glacial erratics and swinging into a switchback that overcomes the steepest pitch.

The remaining distance to Pulpit Rock breezes by in a northward ramble that reaches an unsigned spur path just shy of the halfway mark. An impressive but dangerous outcrop 500 feet above the water, the views of Lake Willoughby's southern end and the cliffs on the western shore make Pulpit Rock a satisfying destination for hikers happy with a shortened route.

Turning away from this midhike outlook, the path scales a 100-yard slope, drifts away from the lake, and climbs vigorously for 0.3 mile. When the pitch gradually eases, scattered stones replace smooth footing in a threadbare trail that bobs and weaves haphazardly a second 0.3 mile to the top. A typical northern forest greets hikers at the summit, but open slabs of exposed ledge just below the absolute peak entertain with a southern panorama of Burke Mountain, Newark Pond, and the central Green Mountain heights.

Even though you've made it to the top, the best is yet to come. The northern end of the Mount Pisgah Trail glances over the peak and descends 2.2 miles reconnecting to Vermont Highway 5A farther up the lake. For views you don't dare miss, follow this less-used northern trail 0.2 mile past the peak and bear left at an obvious spur. A short path drops sharply to boulders at the top of a cliff where views wobble the knees of anyone daring to look straight down. More than 1,000 feet above the highway and the tiny boats that ply the lake, you're standing on the level of Mount Hor's cliffs and higher than Mount Wheeler's face. Scan the length of Lake Willoughby and other highlights snap into view. Count Jay Peak and Mount Mansfield among the distant mountains while Lake Memphremagog gloriously caps the scenery of northern Vermont.

Before backtracking to the trailhead, take a few minutes to visit another outcrop 0.1 mile farther north. More extensive views of the lake's upper lobe are available from this clifftop rock, and patience pays off handsomely if you take your time and relax. I was lucky enough to enjoy bird's-eye views of territorial broad-winged hawks that swooped below the level of my feet and spiraled above my head, defending their space against aerial intruders in remarkable displays of flight.

General description:	A satisfying half-day family hike to lake and mountain views.
General location:	East of Interstate 91 between Saint Johnsbury and Derby Line.
Length:	2.4 miles round-trip.
Difficulty:	Moderate.
Elevation gain:	800 feet.
Special attractions:	Overlook views of Lake Willoughby, Mount Pisgah, and Lake Memphremagog.
Maps:	USGS Sutton quad.
For more information:	Department of Forests, Parks and Recreation, District V, 184 Portland Street, St. Johnsbury, VT 05819; (802) 748-8787.

See Map on Page 185

Finding the trailhead: Follow the directions to Mount Pisgah (see Hike 57). A gravel road leaves the north end of the Mount Pisgah parking lot, bears right at a fork in 0.5 mile, and reaches a parking area for the Herbert Hawkes Trail 1.8 miles from the Pisgah trailhead.

The hike: Hikers put off by crowds at the Pisgah trailhead can find better prospects for unharried walking less than 2 miles up the road. A longer trek to outlooks that lack the pizazz of Mount Pisgah's perches, the Herbert Hawkes Trail to the summit of Mount Hor still caps a pleasant day. For best results, consider this hike on a balmy afternoon when the sun at your back brightens Lake Willoughby's northern reaches and reflects off the rocky cliffs that plunge to its eastern shore.

Thanks to the access road, the Herbert Hawkes Trail steps off from a trailhead already some 700 feet higher than the lake as it pops up stone steps about 20 yards west of the parking lot. Almost immediately the route turns right, easing upward through regenerated forest on an old woods road until it dwindles to a narrow path beneath a steep, eroded slope. After patiently waiting for the angle of the hill to change, the trail turns left on a moderate grade, finally gaining substantial elevation as it ascends through a forest of mature northern hardwoods.

The route becomes temperate again as it twists back to the right, aims a little below the ridge, and halts abruptly at a T where hikers are confronted by directional signs. To the left, the West Branch Trail leads 0.3 mile to Mount Hor's summit and a long-distance western view. To the right, the East Branch Trail runs 0.7 mile to a pair of appealing outlooks high above Lake Willoughby's western shore. Most hikers end up exploring both.

The West Branch Trail pursues a less-traveled course, comfortably maintaining its pace as it rubs past undergrowth that invades the narrow path. After a spur on the right detours to the viewless summit, the route skirts

Lake Willoughby and Mount Hor from Mount Pisgah's Pulpit Rock.

below the peak and ends at a tiny outlook on the mountain's western flank. Most notable within this sunset view are Burke Mountain's summit towers, the corridor of Vermont Highway 5, distant Hazen Notch, and a gaggle of woodland ponds sprinkled beneath your feet.

The East Branch Trail is clearly the more popular prize, a pleasantly level walk below the summit's northern ridge. Passing a small wetland high on the mountain's slopes, this sunny stroll enjoys the songs of birds and breezes in the trees as it lopes to the final payoff, a last fork that guides hikers to alternate lakeside views. A short 75 yards to the right, the east lookout ends in a tree-lined clearing that frames Mount Pisgah's cliffs directly across the water, although much of the lake itself is obscured by growing trees.

The left fork of the East Branch Trail continues 0.1 mile, descending sharply to the north lookout, the highlight of the hike. Lightly curbed by surrounding growth, the panorama from this rocky ledge includes not only a Pisgah view but also a splendid tableau of the heart of the Northeast Kingdom. A mottled landscape of field and forest slants away from Lake Willoughby's bulging shore, the flat gleam of Lake Memphremagog stretches beyond the Canadian border, and the summits of Quebec add depth to far horizons many miles farther north.

57 MOUNT PISGAH AND
58 MOUNT HOR, HERBERT HAWKES TRAIL

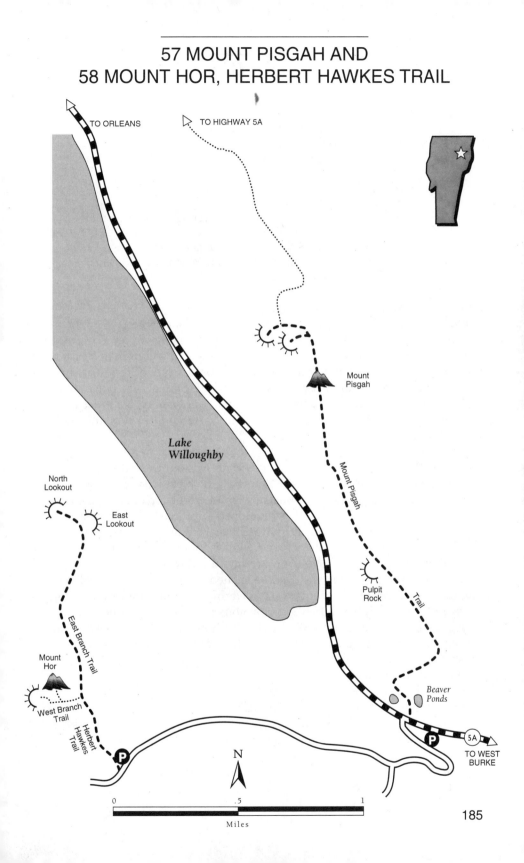

TO ORLEANS

TO HIGHWAY 5A

Mount Pisgah

Mount Pisgah Trail

Lake Willoughby

North Lookout

East Lookout

Pulpit Rock

Mount Hor

East Branch Trail

West Branch Trail

Herbert Hawkes Trail

P

Beaver Ponds

P

5A

TO WEST BURKE

N

0   .5   1

Miles

General description:	A short walk to pristine ponds at the top of the Northeast Kingdom.
General location:	11 miles east of Derby Line, just below the Canadian border.
Length:	4.2 miles round-trip.
Difficulty:	Moderate.
Elevation gain:	100 feet.
Special attractions:	Fishing, wildlife, and overnight shelter on the shore of Round Pond.
Maps:	USGS Morgan Center quad.
For more information:	Department of Fish and Wildlife, 184 Portland Street, St. Johnsbury, VT 05819; (802) 748-8787.

Finding the trailhead: Vermont Highway 111 runs east/west between Derby Center and Vermont Highway 114 north of Island Pond. From either direction, follow VT 111 to Morgan Center and turn north onto Valley Road next to a large parking area at the end of Seymour Lake. Pass a church in Holland Village after 4.5 miles, and continue straight onto a gravel road 0.1 mile later where the paved highway turns sharply left. Stay on the gravel road for 2.9 miles, bear right at a T, and proceed, without turning, 2.3 miles until the road dwindles to one lane and ends at the Vermont Department of Fish and Wildlife Fishing Access at Holland Pond.

The hike: Think of this hike as a nature walk without the frills. No interpretive guides, no trail signs, no route markers, no blazes, no help if you get in trouble—just a broad path to wilderness ponds at the top of the Northeast Kingdom, easily accessible to hikers equipped with map and compass. Remember, though, the Vermont Department of Fish and Wildlife manages this 9,500-acre preserve for its fish and wildlife, not general recreation. Be mindful of the season when you venture into these woods.

Another entrance to this vast tract is located west of Vermont Highway 114, but the Holland Pond section east of Derby Line holds more appeal for the average hiker. Easy walking, conspicuous trails, unspoiled ponds, and an overnight shelter near a brook trout fishing hole makes this northern end of the management area a favored destination. Still, for outdoor folks with the skills to chart a course through big country, any corner of the Bill Sladyk Wildlife Management Area is a marvelous place to roam.

Anyone who doesn't drive a high-clearance, four-wheel-drive vehicle should treat the parking lot for the Holland Pond boat ramp as the trailhead. Walk north on a gravel road that runs off to the left as you enter the parking area and continue straight on a ragged track when the main road swings hard to the right after approximately 0.3 mile. In due course, this pock-marked lane leads to a shaggy clearing, a closed vehicular gate, and a faded sign at what technically is the head of the trail.

59 BILL SLADYK WILDLIFE MANAGEMENT AREA

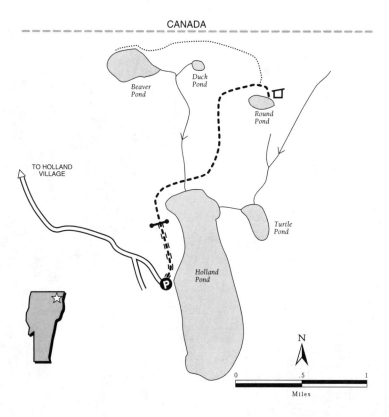

The relaxing junket to Round Pond traces the remnants of an old road that skims over bedrock boulders, shaded by dark green conifers and brilliant hardwoods in the fall. As the broad track jogs northward, a path to Beaver Pond departs on the left while a large expanse of Holland Pond glistens behind a veil of forest on the right. Rounding Holland Pond's northern shore, an inlet sluices over weathered rock bounded by blueberries and cedar trees. The trail then edges a beaver marsh, which you might check for wildlife as you pass. Be careful in the next 0.75 mile. Smaller trails lead into the woods for parts unknown. Keep especially alert soon after the inlet crossing when the track swings north (left) at what may look to some like a confusing fork in the trail. When in doubt, always stick with the well-established, obvious route between Round Pond and the trailhead, and don't be troubled by diverging roads that reconnect around the bend.

A smooth uphill glide ultimately leads to a short spur that reconnoiters Duck Pond as the main trail calmly bumps over a shallow ridge and curls south to an idyllic backcountry camp. Trout seekers and wildlife watchers won't find a better location than the rustic log shelter that sits in a grassy clearing above Round Pond's tranquil shore.

Near the trailhead at Holland Pond.

An optional excursion to Beaver Pond begins on the conspicuous trail that diverges north only 200 yards before the main path reaches the Round Pond shelter. Squeezing through a short aisle of cedars, this less-traveled path circles to the back of Duck Pond and riles up resident partridge on its way to Beaver Pond's northern shore. Only 0.25 mile from the nation's border, the prints of cloven hoofs left in this spongy trail could belong to either American or Canadian moose. Bushwhackers might have fun working their way home by heading south from Beaver Pond. I was content to return to the trailhead by retracing the easy route.

60 WENLOCK WILDLIFE MANAGEMENT AREA, MOOSE BOG

General description:	A short stroll from a state highway to a fragile wilderness wetland.
General location:	Midway between Island Pond and the Connecticut River.
Length:	0.5 mile or 1 mile round trip, depending on where you park.
Difficulty:	Easy.
Elevation gain:	Less than 100 feet.
Special attractions:	Rare and endangered plants; possible sightings of wildlife.
Maps:	Handout maps are available from the address below.
For more information:	Department of Fish and Wildlife, 184 Portland Street, St. Johnsbury, VT 05819; (802) 748-8787.

Finding the trailhead: From the junction of Vermont Highways 114 and 105 in the Town of Island Pond, turn east on VT 105 and drive 8 miles to a railroad crossing. The highway spans the Nulhegan River 0.4 mile after the railroad tracks. Reliable parking is on the left 0.1 mile beyond the river. The trailhead is located on the south side of the highway about 0.25 mile east of the parking area at a rutted four-wheel-drive track where the highway bends to the north. No signs designate the trail. At certain times of the year, it may be possible to park one or two cars off the highway near the trailhead.

The hike: Preserving nearly 2,000 acres in the heart of the Northeast Kingdom, the Wenlock Wildlife Management Area combines fragile Moose Bog with forest and wetland habitats to form an appealingly untamed portion of the Nulhegan River drainage. Statistics tell the tale. In this wild, uncompromising land where human inhabitants are few and far between, snow cover lasts more days than the summer growing season and temperatures can drop to 31 degrees below zero. Vast tracts of spruce-fir forest overwhelm

60 WENLOCK WILDLIFE MANAGEMENT AREA, MOOSE BOG

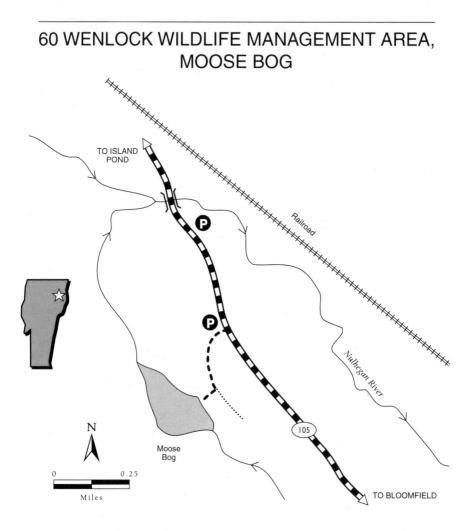

many visitors, who race by on Vermont Highway 105 never knowing that rare plants and endangered species can easily be discovered just a few paces off the road.

A walk to Moose Bog doesn't take much exercise. The entire round trip from the edge of the road is under 0.5 mile. The trail follows a jeep track 70 yards south up a gentle hill to a large boulder that denies vehicular access. Curling left (east) through mossy woodlands of spruce, fir, and birch, an easy stroll leads 0.2 mile to a wide spot in the trail. From this sunny clearing, a smaller path meanders down an easy slope glazed in blueberries and Labrador tea before the trail flattens, peatland provides soft footing, and the sun reflects on the open water of a hidden bog. Wander a few more yards past black spruce and low heath shrubs to the edge of the floating mat. There, hikers are treated to sweeping views of the rolling hills that hold this wetland basin.

The trail is easy to describe; the experience here is not. Much depends on

Rare white moccasin-flowers grace the fringe of Moose Bog.

Blazing rhodora's Moose Bog springtime show.

timing and outright luck. Threatened gray jays, black-backed three-toed woodpeckers, a breeding population of endangered spruce grouse, and other boreal species could surprise the ardent birder, while any hiker should be on the lookout for deer, bear, beaver, and moose that inhabit surrounding terrain. Most people take the time to slowly inspect this environment for natural attractions that are far less fleeting but just as spectacular. In early June, lady's slipper orchids and rare white-moccasin flowers grace the tiny clearing above the bog, while the peatland edge of the floating mat erupts with gaudy phalanxes of red/hot pink rhodora. A variety of unusual wetland plants are always present for examination—pitcher plants, rare climbing ferns, and a personal favorite of mine, the enchanting tamarack. Scattered throughout the wetland scene, spare and random yet precise, the tufted needles of this delicate tree lend to a misty bog the aura of a Japanese garden.

General description:	A scenic half-day mountain hike for families who like to scramble.
General location:	West of Lake Willoughby, between Saint Johnsbury and Derby Line.
Length:	2.1 miles round-trip.
Difficulty:	Moderate.
Elevation gain:	700 feet.
Special attractions:	Barren slabs and rocky outcrops, on a low summit with unusual views.
Maps:	USGS Sutton quad.
For more information:	Department of Forests, Parks and Recreation, District V, 184 Portland Street, St. Johnsbury, VT 05819; (802) 748-8787.

Finding the trailhead: From Exit 23 off Interstate 91, travel 10 miles north on U.S. Highway 5 through Lyndonville to West Burke. Stay on US 5, but note your mileage at the Vermont Highway 5A junction. After 8.6 miles, look for signs to Wheeler Pond camps halfway down a small hill and turn right onto an unmarked gravel road. Drive beyond a parking lot for trails to Wheeler Pond and pass a pair of houses 2 miles from the highway. A parking area will appear on the left about 120 yards past the second house.

Lake Willoughby from the ledges of Wheeler Mountain.

61 WHEELER MOUNTAIN

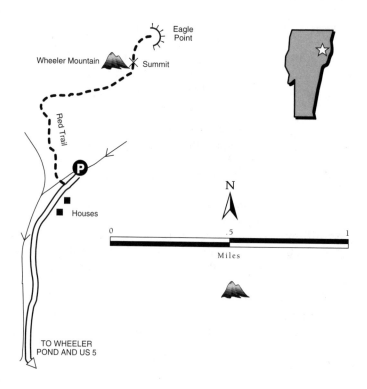

The hike: A few miles west of Lake Willoughby and Mount Pisgah's well-trod cliffs, Wheeler Mountain draws little notice from the usual summer crowds. Its barren slabs, rocky outcrops, and singular summit views remain the unsung province of local hikers in the know. The Red Trail, in particular, attracts savvy north-country parents whose children stretch the limits of family hiking by scrambling over boulders kids naturally seem to love. A scenic, rock-ribbed summit, Wheeler shoulders a big mountain attitude at the end of a moderate trek, and bestows an airy, alpine feeling not common in Vermont.

Begin the climb by backtracking 20 yards down the access road to a small sign at the end of a narrow path that dips through crowding brush and quickly hops a brook. Turning right and curling upward along the edge of a field, the path skims between trees before it suddenly divides. Straight ahead, the White Trail doesn't encounter slabs but it's muddy in spots, harder to follow, and proves to be equally steep. Save it as an escape route in the event of rainy weather.

To the right, the Red Trail scuffles along a well-used course but stirs up a lot more fun. The eroded path runs 50 yards through encroaching woods until the trail widens, red blazes soon appear, and a moderate climb rapidly delivers hikers to a disconcerting slab of rock. Fear not! This hike is scrambly, but it's not suicidal. Keep your wits about you and your eyes on the painted blazes as the route veers and clambers to the top of the frightening slab, aided on occasion by handholds and better footing at the edge of the path.

As you ease onto the lip of the steepest ledge, a great view of Wheeler Pond opens behind your back. The White Trail returns on the left, noted by faded blazes and an arrow on a withered tree. The combined trails swing right (easterly) away from the open slabs to ascend through evergreens, but hikers should first circle left to the highest point of a rocky mound where vistas reveal the northern Green Mountains and the summit of Jay Peak.

Only minor scrambles impede progress as the trail rises through woods that rim the summit's southern flank. A brief descent then steadies the route for a marvelous 70-yard stroll along an open humpbacked spine where the notches of nearby peaks frame more southerly mountain views. Even though you're near the top, don't assume you're at the end. Stick with the path that ducks below the summit and skitters to an eastern cliff for the best view of the hike. This short descent through conifers leads to Eagle Point, a wondrous vista over forest and farm to Lake Willoughby's slender form, embraced as it has been since the Ice Age by Mount Pisgah and Mount Hor.

APPENDIX A
USDA Forest Service Offices

Forest Supervisor
Green Mountain National Forest
231 North Main Street
Rutland, VT 05701
(802) 747-6700

Manchester Ranger District
Routes 11 and 30
RR 1, Box 1940
Manchester Center, VT 05255
(802) 362-2307

Middlebury Ranger District
Route 7
RR 4, Box 1260
Middlebury, VT 05753
(802) 388-4362

Rochester Ranger District
Route 100
RR 2, Box 35
Rochester, VT 05767
(802) 767-4261

APPENDIX B
Vermont Agency of Natural Resources

Department of Forests, Parks and
Recreation
103 South Main Street, 10 South
Waterbury, VT 05671-0601
(802) 241-3655

District Offices

District I - Southeast
RR 1, Box 33
North Springfield, VT 05150
(802) 886-2215

District II - Southwest
RR 2, Box 2161
Pittsford, VT 05763-9713
(802) 483-2314

District III - Northwest
111 West Street
Essex Junction, VT 05452
(802) 879-6565

District IV - Central
324 North Main Street
Barre, VT 05641
(802) 479-3241

District V - Northeast Kingdom
184 Portland Street
St. Johnsbury, VT 05819
(802) 748-8787

ABOUT THE AUTHOR

Enthusiastically combining a professional career with freelance writing, outdoor photography, and avid exploration, Larry Pletcher brings twenty-three years of hiking experience to the trailheads of Vermont. Whether bagging peaks in the White and Green mountains, rambling through forests near his foothills home, or canoeing with his family, Larry has amassed innumerable miles of backcountry travel throughout New England and eastern Canada. He is the author and photographer of *Hiking New Hampshire*, also published by Falcon Press.

FALCON GUIDES ®Leading the way™

FalconGuides® are available for where-to-go hiking, mountain biking, rock climbing, walking, scenic driving, fishing, rockhounding, paddling, birding, wildlife viewing, and camping. We also have FalconGuides on essential outdoor skills and subjects and field identification. The following titles are currently available, but this list grows every year. For a free catalog with a complete list of titles, call FALCON toll-free at 1-800-582-2665.

HIKING GUIDES

Best Hikes Along the Continental Divide
Hiking Alaska
Hiking Arizona
Hiking Arizona's Cactus Country
Hiking the Beartooths
Hiking Big Bend National Park
Hiking the Bob Marshall Country
Hiking California
Hiking California's Desert Parks
Hiking Carlsbad Caverns
    and Guadalupe Mtns. National Parks
Hiking Colorado
Hiking Colorado, Vol. II
Hiking Colorado's Summits
Hiking Colorado's Weminuche Wilderness
Hiking the Columbia River Gorge
Hiking Florida
Hiking Georgia
Hiking Glacier & Waterton Lakes National Parks
Hiking Grand Canyon National Park
Hiking Grand Staircase-Escalante/Glen Canyon
Hiking Grand Teton National Park
Hiking Great Basin National Park
Hiking Hot Springs in the Pacific Northwest
Hiking Idaho
Hiking Indiana
Hiking Maine
Hiking Maryland and Delaware
Hiking Michigan
Hiking Minnesota
Hiking Montana
Hiking Mount Rainier National Park
Hiking Mount St. Helens
Hiking Nevada
Hiking New Hampshire
Hiking New Mexico

Hiking New Mexico's Gila Wilderness
Hiking New York
Hiking North Carolina
Hiking the North Cascades
Hiking Northern Arizona
Hiking Northern California
Hiking Olympic National Park
Hiking Oregon
Hiking Oregon's Eagle Cap Wilderness
Hiking Oregon's Mount Hood/Badger Creek
Hiking Oregon's Central Cascades
Hiking Pennsylvania
Hiking Ruins Seldom Seen
Hiking Shenandoah
Hiking the Sierra Nevada
Hiking South Carolina
Hiking South Dakota's Black Hills Country
Hiking Southern New England
Hiking Tennessee
Hiking Texas
Hiking Utah
Hiking Utah's Summits
Hiking Vermont
Hiking Virginia
Hiking Washington
Hiking Wisconsin
Hiking Wyoming
Hiking Wyoming's Cloud Peak Wilderness
Hiking Wyoming's Teton and Washakie Wilderness
Hiking Wyoming's Wind River Range
Hiking Yellowstone National Park
Hiking Yosemite National Park
Hiking Zion & Bryce Canyon National Parks
Wild Country Companion
Wild Montana
Wild Utah
Wild Virginia

■ *To order any of these books, check with your local bookseller*
*or call FALCON ® at **1-800-582-2665**.*
Visit us on the world wide web at:
www.Falcon.com

FALCON®

FALCON GUIDES ® Leading the Way™

FIELD GUIDES
Bitterroot: Montana State Flower
Canyon Country Wildflowers
Central Rocky Mountains
   Wildflowers
Chihuahuan Desert Wildflowers
Great Lakes Berry Book
New England Berry Book
Ozark Wildflowers
Pacific Northwest Berry Book
Plants of Arizona
Rare Plants of Colorado
Rocky Mountain Berry Book
Scats & Tracks of the Pacific
   Coast States
Scats & Tracks of the
   Rocky Mountains
Sierra Nevada Wildflowers
Southern Rocky Mountain
   Wildflowers
Tallgrass Prairie Wildflowers
Western Trees
Wildflowers of Southwestern
   Utah

FISHING GUIDES
Fishing Alaska
Fishing the Beartooths
Fishing Florida
Fishing Georgia
Fishing Glacier National Park
Fishing Maine
Fishing Montana
Fishing Wyoming
Fishing Yellowstone
   National Park
Trout Unlimited's Guide to
   America's 100 Best Trout
   Streams
America's Best Bass Fishing

BIRDING GUIDES
Birding Georgia
Birding Illinois
Birding Minnesota
Birding Montana
Birding Northern California
Birding Texas
Birding Utah

MORE GUIDEBOOKS
Backcountry Horseman's
   Guide to Washington
Camping Arizona
Camping California's
   National Forests
Camping Colorado
Camping Oregon
Exploring Canyonlands &
   Arches National Parks
Exploring Hawaii's Parklands
Exploring Mount Helena
Exploring Southern California
   Beaches
Family Fun in Montana
Family Fun in Yellowstone
Hiking Hot Springs of the Pacific
   Northwest
Recreation Guide to WA
   National Forests
Touring Arizona Hot Springs
Touring California & Nevada
   Hot Springs
Touring Colorado Hot Springs
Touring Montana & Wyoming
   Hot Springs
Trail Riding Western Montana
Wilderness Directory
Wild Montana
Wild Utah
Wild Virginia

ROCKHOUNDING GUIDES
Rockhounding Arizona
Rockhounding California
Rockhounding Colorado
Rockhounding Montana
Rockhounding Nevada
Rockhound's Guide to New
   Mexico
Rockhounding Texas
Rockhounding Utah
Rockhounding Wyoming

HOW-TO GUIDES
Avalanche Aware
Backpacking Tips
Bear Aware
Desert Hiking Tips
Hiking with Dogs
Hiking with Kids
Leave No Trace
Mountain Lion Alert
Reading Weather
Route Finding
Using GPS
Wild Country Companion
Wilderness First Aid
Wilderness Survival

WALKING
Walking Colorado Springs
Walking Denver
Walking Portland
Walking Seattle
Walking St. Louis
Walking San Francisco
Walking Virginia Beach

■*To order any of these books, check with your local bookseller
or call FALCON ® at **1-800-582-2665**.
Visit us on the world wide web at:
www.falcon.com*

FALCON®

American Hiking Society

American Hiking Society is the only national nonprofit organization dedicated to establishing, protecting and maintaining foot trails in America.

Establishing...

American Hiking Society establishes hiking trails with the AHS National Trails Endowment, providing grants for grassroots organizations to purchase trail lands, construct and maintain trails, and preserve hiking trails' scenic values. The AHS affiliate club program, called the Congress of Hiking Organizations, brings trail clubs together to share information, collaborate on public policy, and advocate legislation and policies that protect hiking trails.

Protecting...

American Hiking Society protects hiking trails through highly focused public policy efforts in the nation's capital. AHS affects federal legislation, shapes public lands policy, collaborates with grassroots trail organizations, and partners with federal land managers to protect the hiking experience. Members become active with letter-writing campaigns and by attending the annual AHS Trails Advocacy Week.

Maintaining...

American Hiking Society maintains hiking trails by sending volunteers to national parks, forests and recreation lands; organizing volunteer teams to help affiliated hiking clubs; and publishing national volunteer directories. AHS members get involved, get dirty and get inspired by participating in AHS programs like National Trails Day, America's largest celebration of the outdoors; and Volunteer Vacations—week-long work trips to beautiful, wild places.

Join American Hiking Society...

Be a part of the organization dedicated to protecting and preserving the nation's footpaths, our footpaths, the ones in our backyards and our backcountry. Visit American Hiking Society's website or call to find out more about membership. When you join, Falcon Publishing will send you a FREE guide as a special thank you for contributing to the efforts of American Hiking Society.

American Hiking Society
1422 Fenwick Lane
Silver Spring, MD 20910
OR CALL: (888) 766-HIKE ext. 1
OR VISIT: www.americanhiking.org